Advance Praise for

The Most Reverend Earl Boyea, Auxiliary Bishop of Detroit

How can suffering benefit someone else let alone me? Redemptive suffering is at the heart of the Christian faith: Christ's death is of eternal benefit to all of us. Further, any linking of our own sufferings with that sublime offering of Christ also brings benefit. How is it that we can claim this? Only by faith. Cathy Adamkiewicz writes movingly of the birth, life, and death of her third daughter, seventh child. And it has been a redemptive life. Cathy demonstrates the fruitfulness of a solid Catholic faith: not only has it been productive in the lives of seven wonderful children; not only is it clearly a counter-sign to the contraceptive world view so prevalent these days; but it also can cause a father, Aaron, to carry that small coffin to the altar as an offering which transforms those who witness. Cathy has written a story infused with her own baptismal virtues: faith, hope, and, what will last forever, love.

Kimberly Hahn, author of *Chosen and Cherished: Biblical Wisdom for Your Marriage*

By sharing her journey of faith through the heartbreaking loss of her daughter, Cathy reveals the heart of God: he brings joy in the midst of sorrow, peace in the center of trial, and love in the depth of loss. She shares the richness of the purpose of each life, which is part of the legacy her daughter leaves us all. Highly recommended.

Patti Armstrong,
Co-author of "The Amazing Grace" series

Broken and Blessed is a story of a Mother's pain of having an infant born with serious health problems. By sharing this deeply personal journey, Catherine provides understanding, support and strength to anyone who must watch helplessly as a precious loved one struggles for life. Catherine takes the reader beyond mere events and into the spiritual realm where true healing requires coming to terms with a God who chooses our path in life in spite of our protests when the burden feels too heavy. Yet, even in the midst of pain, Catherine finds laughter, joy and little celebrations, and still, she finda peace with God.

Patti Monroe-Mohrenweiser,
parent of a heart surgery survivor

Honestly, I'm speechless. This book doesn't have a specific market, because *everybody* is in the market. Everybody needs to read this book. I want my prayer group to read it. I want my husband to read it. I want my friends to read it. I want my daughter to read it. This is the first time I've actually seen a way to get through to her so that she will view her 'ordeal' as a blessing.

Janine Edwards, chaplain,
Kaleidoscope Kids (Hospice for children, Detroit)

Your story is special and needs to be told. Personally, this helps me as a chaplain and your perspective helps me in my dealings with other parents. I appreciate your ability to be honest about your true thoughts and feelings. That takes guts. This story is very important.

Dr. Mark Latkovic, Professor of Moral Theology, Sacred Heart Major Seminary, Detroit

Because your story is at once intimately personal, yet universal, I believe that your audience is a broad one – Catholic, Protestant, Jew, Muslim, even non-religious. It has much to teach about not just suffering and death, but the meaning of life.

For my children

Broken and Blessed

A Life Story

Catherine Adamkiewicz

© 2007 by Catherine Adamkiewicz

Cover Artwork © 2007 by Patti Monroe-Mohrenweiser

Portrait of Jesus and Celeste © 2005 Tracy Christianson

Printed in the United States of America

All rights reserved. No part of this publication may be reproduced, stored in a retrieval system, or transmitted in any form or by any means-for example, electronic, photocopy, recording-without the prior written permission of the author. The only exception is brief quotations in printed reviews.

Published by
Bezalel Books, Waterford, MI
Please visit our website for the finest in Christian fiction and non-fiction books
www.BezalelBooks.com

ISBN 978-0-9794976-6-7
Library of Congress Control Number 2007933657

An Invitation

"I've often said that when you're faced with a decision, it's usually best to take the more difficult route, since that is usually the right way to go. Letting go of Celeste was the most difficult thing I've ever done. To me, Celeste represented hope, and if I let her go, I thought I was giving up hope. But then I came to understand that I needed to let her go, not for me or for her, but to show that God's will is perfect. I know He had a plan for her."
Aaron Adamkiewicz,
Celeste's beloved daddy

This is the story of a beautiful child, perfectly planned by God, and the work she was brought here to accomplish. It is also the story of a family touched by her presence and of a community transformed by lifting her up in prayer. It is

An Invitation

the story of a mother who learned to trust God and to accept His will with a grace that can only be called miraculous. It is a story of faith, love, and even joy in the face of sadness and pain.

Very few people actually met Celeste. But her influence was far-reaching. Why? Because, as we are fond of saying, she got the job done. She completed the task of life in record speed, touching the lives of so many simply by *being*. Could it be that simple? Could it be that Celeste was sent to us not just to be our little girl, to wear pink dresses and go to Daddy Daughter Date Night, but to *preach the gospel*?

This is the amazing and tender story of how she did just that. I invite you to meet Celeste and allow her to bless your heart, as she did ours.

The Seventh Moment

"God Who is mighty has done great things for me, and holy is His Name."
Luke 1:49

She is about to be born. It is after eleven on the night of March 14, 2005, and I have been in a gentle sort of labor all day. The doctors have decided a cesarean is the best option now, because the baby's heart tones are not "bouncing back" the way they should after each contraction.

I am not afraid. I am so anxious to see her. My labor has not been difficult or particularly eventful. Though induced, I have not felt many very painful contractions. I have been through this before, six times in fact, and I know what to expect. This will be my second c-section. They will make the incision and my beautiful child will be lifted from my womb. They will hold her up (please God, let it be a girl!) and she will be chubby and pink. She will cry and I will cry and her father will cry, and soon I will hold her, and with so much joy draw her to my breast to nurse her for the first time. Yes, I have been through this before. Those six births are so close in my memory now, the six most miraculous moments of my life. The six moments so full of joy it is difficult to describe them. And so I wait for the seventh moment, fully expecting the bliss I have come to take for granted, the bliss all mothers greet with such eagerness after nine months, with anxious anticipation.

Like most of my other children, she was not "planned" by me, but by Someone else. At seven months into my pregnancy, I celebrated my 40th birthday. In some ways I felt I was getting too old for this. Our small home was already crowded with two nearly grown girls and four active boys. We had been going through a challenging time in our marriage, a season of growth and pain; in the eyes of most, this was a bad time to get pregnant. But since early in our marriage, we had chosen to be open to the will of God regarding the number of children we would welcome. So it seems He had decided this was indeed a good time to have a baby.

Our other children certainly thought so. We had raised them with the thinking that the best gifts God had to give came in the form of babies, and they believed it. Rachel, our eldest at 18, was a freshman at the Franciscan University of Steubenville. It was a big adjustment for her, living away from home for the first time. This was the first time she would be absent for the birth of a sibling, and she was missing us. Tall and dramatic, our Rachel was sensitive and talkative, my only brown-eyed child. She reminded me a lot of myself at her age. It was funny to think that I was expecting a baby while my eldest was only a bit younger than I was back in '86, when she was born.

Rachel's younger sister by sixteen months, Lauren, was a precocious and industrious seventeen-year-old. Finishing up her senior year of home schooling, she was anxious to begin nursing school. Lauren had a part-time job, a boyfriend, and lots of friends. She was looking forward to having a new baby sister. After four baby brothers, a little girl in the family was her fantasy. I can't count how many times Lauren would beg me for a younger sister, from the time she was quite young. She loved her brothers, but she so wanted a baby girl. A self-professed "girly-girl," she dreamed about selecting outfits and styling hair.

Alexander, more commonly called A.J., headed up the pack of boys. He was 13 that spring, and he was really "growing into himself." He had added six inches in height that past year, and he was turning into a man. I often told people he was my right arm. He helped me around the house in so many ways, doing everything from putting together baby furniture to cooking dinner. He had a special habit of going out of his way to notice the needs of others; he had a true servant's heart. He was the one to make sure I took time to rest, the one who carried groceries for me and brought me tea or water as a special way to care me. He frequently helped out with his younger brothers, even changing diapers! When his youngest brother was born, I called A.J. his baby nurse, as he was the one to give him the occasional bottle or dose of medicine. He was so happy to be awaiting a new baby to care for.

Ten-year-old Joey was the athlete of the family. He loved sports, particularly soccer. I had never known a child to be so committed to the teams on which he played. He hated to be late for anything, sighing and shaking his head at my tardiness to his games. He also had a mature faith and a love of all things Catholic. His soccer coach picked up on that and named him the team's "spiritual captain," asking him to lead them in prayer before games. It says something about Joey's character that I did not hear about this from him, but from his coach, many months later. The family spoke often about Joey's future vocation, claiming him the family priest. He has never argued with that.

My five-year-old, John, was a smart, handsome Mama's boy. I don't think a boy ever loved his mom the way that John loved me! Those five years in between Joey and John had made me quite a doting mother by the time he came along, and in many ways he was the little prince. He loved books and had me reading three stories to him every night at bedtime. (Not two or four, mind you, it had to be three.) By that winter I was convinced I had read every children's book known to man three or four times, but still we read them again! I think mostly he wanted that time with Mama, and in fact it was special to me, too. He wanted a new baby, if that's what I wanted, but I don't think he was too excited to be sharing me yet again. It was bad enough that he had to share me with Luke.

Lukie, the baby, was almost three. What an adorable, charming boy was Lukie Norman! I joked that if you looked up "cute baby" in the dictionary, you found Luke. His tawny curls and big blue eyes melted everyone's heart, which was good because he was a bit mischievous, as three-year-old boys tend to be. Everyone doted on him, of course, because who wouldn't? He was too little to understand much about waiting for the baby, but each night he'd cuddle next to me, his chubby hands on my belly, and command his sister to move, giggling when she did. I was anxious to see the two of them together, and soon. I knew there'd be a few obstacles here and there, but that was also part of the beauty of a growing family. God provides some of His most anointed blessings in our challenges. It would be breathtaking and joyful even while it was tiring and demanding.

There's no question that my husband thought it was going to be wonderful. Aaron thought everything was wonderful! After almost 20 years of marriage, I knew him well enough to say with certainty that the world had never seen a man with a more positive attitude. I'd also never known one who loved children more, especially these children. He liked his job as a credit union vice president, enjoyed gardening, and was passionate about football, but he *loved* his family. A new addition to his clan put him in seventh heaven, pun intended.

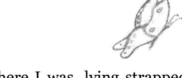

Now here I was, lying strapped in cruciform in the operating room of St. Mary's Hospital. I am not one to chant bible verses, especially while in labor, so I puzzled at the frequency with which this paraphrase of Luke kept entering my mind: "God Who is mighty has done great things for me, and holy is His Name." Again and again it played in my thoughts, like a song heard one time too many, as I waited for the doctor to make the incision that would bring my perfect baby into our imperfect world.

Then she was there. I believe she cried, softly, and I know I did. I took a look at her, stunned by her tiny-ness, surprised at how unlike my other children she appeared. Yes, she was indeed a little girl! "Celeste, everything about you is a surprise," I whispered. How little did I know that the surprises had just begun. I had no idea at that moment where the next four months would lead us. I had no idea how profound would be the suffering, how excruciating the joy, how complete the transformation. I had no idea how truly mighty my God was, or how great would be the works He would accomplish through my little Celeste and me. I did not know how this child would lead me to bask in awe at His holiness, and how I would wonder at my ability to endure such trials and continue to breathe. The adventure of Celeste's life had begun.

The nurses began to do the things nurses do upon the arrival of a newborn. They quickly weighed her; six pounds, four ounces. So incredibly small! Most of my other children had been over 10 pounds. My other c-section, my fourth child, Joey, weighed in at almost eleven pounds! And here was tiny Celeste, not at all chubby, and well, not quite pink either. I was waiting for the nurse to quickly swaddle her and hold her up to my face so I could get a closer look. Aaron snapped a few pictures of her, and one nurse quietly announced she was taking the baby to the nursery. She was going to give her "just a bit" of oxygen. I was still not afraid. It did not occur to me that anything could be truly wrong. I figured she would be there for a short while, and they would bring her quickly back to me.

After closing my incision, they prepared to wheel me to the recovery room. I asked Aaron to get my rosary. I was still not terribly concerned, just disappointed that I had not yet been able to hold Celeste. As we waited anxiously in the recovery room, we couldn't help but overhear the conversation of the neonatologist and the woman in the bed next to me. It seemed her baby, a little boy born just moments before Celeste, was in serious condition. They were asking the parents if they wanted to send him to The University of Michigan Hospital, or the Children's Hospital in Detroit, as St. Mary's did not have a neonatal intensive care unit. I was overcome with concern for that little boy, and began to pray my rosary for him. Thank God, I thought, that our baby isn't sick like that.

Just a few moments later the same doctor appeared near the foot of my bed. As he began to speak I started to correct him, telling him he was at the wrong bedside. I was sure he was here to talk to the poor mother next to me. By now I had overheard that she had already had one stillborn child, and that her newborn was in serious danger. The doctor smiled and made some comment about my looking familiar to him. I wondered why he was taking so long to get to that other mother, when the reason was at last revealed.

"We believe your baby has a heart defect," I heard him say. "We're wondering which hospital you'd like her sent to," he continued. Aaron and I looked at each other, unbelieving. The doctor explained that they had done an x-ray of Celeste's heart, which indicated it was quite enlarged. "If you're wondering if your baby is going to die tonight, don't worry," he assured us. "It's just best we send her where they can do a heart echo and find out what's wrong."

He left as quickly as he had appeared, and we were left alone, stunned. We had no idea anything was wrong with our baby. My pregnancy had been, after all, uneventful. Aside from a slight rise in my blood pressure these last few days, I had felt well, and a routine ultrasound at 18 weeks had indicated nothing of concern. Now they were taking my baby away to another hospital, and I had not even held her yet. I had been robbed of my seventh moment. I began to pray my rosary for Celeste. And for myself, that I could make it through that first night without her. As I began to cry, the nurses attending me assured me that everything was going to be fine. I'll never forget the words of one of them: "You are going to have so much fun with that baby!" I held onto those words so tightly that night, held on to them for dear life.

Around 3 a.m. the transport team from Children's Hospital arrived. Numbly, I sent home Lauren with my mother, who had come to witness Celeste's birth. They had been disappointed that I needed a c-section, which meant they would be denied the opportunity of seeing our new baby come into the world. When we told them about the heart concerns, these disappointments paled in comparison to the worry that took root.

I had just gone through major surgery and was about to send my newborn baby off without me. I felt overwhelmed with fear. How could this be happening? It was a question I would ask frequently in the days and weeks to come. When the transport team entered my room with Celeste, tiny and naked in that giant plastic box, I tried to get myself together as best as I could. As I reached through the small whole in the unit's side to touch her for the first time, I fought back tears and faked a smile as they snapped a few photos of us. *Are they taking our picture because I may never see her again?* I wondered. They swiftly shuttled her out of the room, their smiles never fading. They were good at this. They did this all the time.

They took newborn infants away from their mothers on the night of their birth, whisking them off into the darkness on whirlwind ambulance rides. For them, it was all in a night's work. For me, it was the beginning of one of the darkest nights of my life.

The remaining details of that night I've forgotten or buried too deeply to be excavated. I believe God has allowed me episodes of merciful amnesia to protect me from the harshness of the most painful of my experiences. I know I was exhausted, both physically and spiritually, and I know I was granted some sleep that night. It was the first of many surreal experiences. I had given birth, but there was no baby at my breast. It was such a foreign feeling. I began to pray in earnest, the repetitive prayers of the rosary and the chaplet of divine mercy: the prayers of my youth. When that became too difficult, I simply spoke quietly, again and again, "Jesus, I trust in You." Like never before, I was thankful for my Catholic faith.

My Catholic faith is as much a part of me as my brown eyes and chubby thighs, and like those attributes I've had it since birth. I'm what they call a "cradle Catholic." I was raised in a family observant and orthodox, if not devout. Weekly Mass attendance and grace before meals framed our faith experience as a family. We attempted to arrive early for the recitation of the rosary, the traditional Catholic prayers honoring the mother of Jesus, that preceded each mass at our parish church. My parents, who had my brother and I late in life, assumed that we were being trained well in our faith at the weekly CCD classes we attended. Instead, we were the unfortunate victims of that post-Vatican II well-intentioned experiment in faith formation.

Unfortunately, like many of our generation, we were merely trained in the sloppy creation of collages and poor renditions of "Kumbaya." Yes, we knew how amazing we were and how much God loved us, but following the Commandments, the Beatitudes, and the teachings of the church kind of got lost at the bottom of the "feel-good" heap. Remarkably, I managed to hang on to some scrap of desire to find out what this religion business was really about. Like all young people, I craved the challenge of the truth. It took many years, lots of searching, and more than a small share of grace to lead me to a real understanding of what my church taught and whether or not I would choose to believe it.

The path to true faith, for me, was a rocky one. Although I never stopped attending Mass, I strayed from true practice for most of my teen years. I sought what I felt was lacking in my family life in the culture at large. Even though my conscience told me to run the other way, I gave in to the immorality demanded of me by my peers. I began a descent into the world which began with alcohol and ended with the birth of my first child a month before I married her father. I know now the grace of God was already powerfully at work in me even then. My pregnancy with Rachel became a catalyst. I looked inside myself and asked an important question. "Who will you become?" I turned to God for the strength to get through this trauma; in return I promised to seek the wisdom to do the right thing. I began to look forward instead of back. Because of His faithfulness, I was granted the strength I required, and my journey into an adult Christian life began. And now here I was, 20 years later, sold out to the Lord, blessed by Him beyond measure, being asked by Him to pick up a heavy cross. Indeed, I was thankful for my Catholic faith.

But of course, faith without works is dead. It would take action to carry this cross, to accept this suffering. It would take virtues I lacked. Strength without ceasing. It would take much more than faith.

Three Days

*"Faithless is he who says farewell
when the road darkens."*
J.R.R. Tolkien

It would take more than faith to get me to that first morning in the hospital without Celeste. It would take the quiet concern of a staff of dedicated nurses. It would take the strength of a wonderful husband, weary with fear for his little girl's life. It would take the love of family, and the concrete support of friends. It took more than I could have imagined, more than I would've hoped for just hours before.

The next few days in the hospital are a blur. My

well-meaning parents brought my children to visit, but it was almost more than I could bear. We have a tradition in our family in which each child is photographed with his or her new sibling, beginning with the youngest child, who is experiencing being a big brother or sister for the first time. It was so painful to hold my three-year-old, Luke, and tell him he would have to wait to see his new baby sister. I was empty in all ways, and having the whole family there felt like more of a burden than a comfort.

There were some moments of consolation. Dear friends came to visit on my second night there, bearing precious gifts of chocolate chip cookies and conversation. We laughed, we actually laughed. They told stories that had nothing to do with sick babies, and we escaped the awful reality for a brief time. They assured me that Celeste would be fine, as of course they should have, even though we all knew we had no idea what would happen. At this point we didn't even know the extent of her heart damage, only that it did indeed have a name: Ebstein's Anomaly.

I would become very familiar with this rare defect in the months to come, but at this point all I knew was that my perfect baby was not perfect, at least by most standards. It seems Ebstein's, which is a malformation of the tricuspid valve, is present at birth but not usually diagnosed until adulthood. We didn't know it yet, but Celeste had a very severe case. The information that the doctors gave Aaron, and what he could gather from the Internet, made us feel that she would be fine. Surgery may be necessary, but maybe not until she was a teenager. Most frequently we noted the primary caution for Ebstein's patients was to take antibiotics before dental procedures. Gosh, that ain't nothin'! This can't be *that* serious.

    We tried to smile and reassure ourselves to the point of exhaustion. I remember clearly the phone call from my beloved husband that first morning. He had been with the baby at Children's, and had spoken to one of the staff cardiologists. Aaron's voice was especially calm as he told me the name of Celeste's defect and tried to describe it. His attempt at cheerfulness was gallant, but I knew him too well. He was terrified. He was comforted by the fact that the doctor was a Catholic -- and one who was not afraid to share his faith. The wise physician counseled that we place Celeste in our Blessed Mother's hands, and that everything would be fine. More precious words of hope to hold onto. But of course, being human, we were afraid, and we wanted to know why this was happening to our precious baby. I knew I was breaking "the rule" but I couldn't help it. "The rule?"

    We have a rule around our house. Well, we have several rules, some of them silly (don't eat the cat food), most of them useful (don't wear muddy shoes in the house) and all of them commonly ignored. But this one's my favorite: NO "why" questions are allowed.

It started, like all good compulsions, in my childhood. My mother has always had a tendency to ask "Why?" – frequently. "Why are those toys scattered all over the floor?" she'd ask. "Why didn't the store have that item in stock?" "Why do people make such poor choices?" Logical to a fault, she knew there were reasons for everything. I was more emotional and impulsive, she, by temperament and training, a fanatic for asking and answering "Why?" She was Spock to my Kirk, and it drove me mad. In the home of my youth, why's were encouraged. In *my* home, as an act of rebellion, I forbade the question. Ask "how?" and "where?" and even "what in the world?" all you want. Just forget about why.

When you have a sick child, you ask why. You wonder for a moment about genetics and environment, and ponder if there was anything you or anyone else could have done to prevent this. Honestly, I didn't think about this long. I broke the rule and then I let it go. My habit of avoiding this question had led to the realization that even if I knew why, I couldn't change the past. It was useless to spend time there. I moved quickly to the "Big Why Question," the one shouted to a god who was supposed to love me. **Why did this happen to my child?**

I was a good mother who wanted children. I tried to be a faithful Christian. Was God punishing me? Testing me? It didn't seem fair, and I quickly came to terms that there's a reason for that. *It wasn't fair.* Pain and suffering and evil are *not* fair. They just *are*. I knew that my faith taught clearly on these matters. I understood that the Old Testament, in particular, was filled with stories of righteous believers who endured all sorts of calamities. A little Job, anyone? And Jesus was frequently asked why so-and-so was suffering a particular affliction—"Did he sin, or was it his parents?" Jesus steered the curious around to the truth, of course: that suffering in life is not necessarily a punishment for sin. Could it truly be more than that? Could it be an opportunity for growth, a necessary purging, a path to heaven, in fact a *gift*?

I did my share of fist shaking to Heaven, don't be fooled. But in the quiet of my heart I knew the answer to my self-forbidden question.

"Why?"

"Why not?!?"

That's right, why not? Why not me, why not my baby?

Was there a child in Children's Hospital who deserved to be there? Was there a parent who had done some evil so great as to warrant such a punishment for an innocent baby?

Of course not. Why questions are all right, I suppose, if we ask the right ones. Asking why God was allowing this was only helpful if I saw it from the right perspective, His perspective. There could never be a sufficient answer in human terms. It became important to determine *His* why. If He truly loved me, and I earnestly believed He did, there was a reason for all this. "All things for the good of those who love Him." I did love Him, and I had to learn to trust, to accept that this experience was the best thing in the world for all of us. Not an easy task. But the alternative, the endless asking why, was not for me. I said "Why not?" and let myself fall, waiting for Him to catch me. Sort of a cosmic trust game.

You might ask why I would do such a thing and I would have to respond, "Why not?"

So as we asked those age-old questions, trying to comprehend the depth of the journey that lay before us, I anxiously awaited escape from the hospital. Because I was so eager to see my daughter, who was now at Children's Hospital, my doctor told me I could be released Thursday morning, if all went well. Meanwhile Aaron and the children alternated between visits to me in one hospital and visits to our dear baby at another hospital. They brought me photos that the nurses took of them with their new sister.

They didn't seem too concerned, even the teenagers; but then again, why should they? Didn't things always turn out all right? I wept as I looked at the pictures, seeing each in turn holding her, and realizing that this moment, too, had been taken from me. They did not allow Luke to hold his sister, so our tradition had to be delayed. Would I be denied all happiness with Celeste? Would all the joy I had expected with her be taken from me? Satan whispered suggestions of despair and fear and I spent the first few days of Celeste's life fighting against the temptation to succumb to these feelings. Ultimately, honestly, I spent most of Celeste's life, with God's grace, resisting that dark place where physical and emotional exhaustion wanted to take me. I began to focus on God's promises to me, on His goodness and His mercy. I formulated a new mantra: God is in control. I began the process of giving Celeste back to Him, a process that continues to this day.

Intensive Care

"May Thy grace, O Lord, make that possible to me which seems impossible to me by nature."
Thomas a Kempis, Imitation of Christ

It is a long hallway. You walk though a set of double doors. To your right are four offices. Rarely do you see anyone exit or enter them. On that same wall, between the offices, are large black and white portraits of intelligent-looking women in white coats: the doctors. The walls were formerly a nondescript shade of cream, but that same summer they were repainted yellow. A cheerful color. When you get to the end of the hall you must push a button that alerts the staff at the desk that a visitor has arrived. They push the signal button that unlocks the doors. You enter, and then you wash.

You wash and you wash and you wash. You wash because here, as nowhere else, germs are the enemy. You tear open the little sponge containing the disinfectant soap, and you scrub your arms up to the elbows. If you are obedient, if you are a good parent, you look up at the clock and scrub for a full three minutes, as directed. After you visit a few times, you realize that the scrubby things run out on occasion. That's ok. You discover they are kept in the cupboard to the right. Nothing changes much here. That's why that yellow paint was such a surprise.

But on your first night here it is all new. It is a long hallway. The photos of the doctors are a little scary. You know that your baby is somewhere on the other side of those double doors, and three minutes of scrubbing is a long time. I imagine they are all a bit like this, the NICUs of the world. The neonatal intensive care units of children's hospitals. Places we are all glad exist. Places we never want to visit.

I held my daughter in my arms for the first time on the evening of March 17. I did not walk down the long hallway. Instead, Aaron pushed me in a wheelchair, as I was having a hard time walking following surgery. It was a difficult trip, but not the hardest one I'd made that day. That morning I had left St. Mary's without my baby. It was a beautiful day, sunny and bright. The ride would have been lovely under normal circumstances. The route home took us down scenic Hines Drive, a winding road that passes through several communities bordering on the Rouge River. I wept the whole way. It was beyond my comprehension to be leaving the hospital without my daughter, to be carting home a hospital-grade breast pump, the car seat in the trunk. But no baby, no baby.

I was so anxious to get to the hospital, but first I had to stop at home to see the other children and to try out the ubiquitous breast pump. Aaron and the children had put up signs on the front of the house: It's a Girl! A message that should have filled me with joy only compounded my pain. My so longed-for little girl was here, but not in my arms where she belonged.

The trip to Children's Hospital was only about 20 minutes long, but of course it seemed endless. It was a trip I would make more than 100 times, but I didn't know that yet. The drill would become so familiar, numbingly so. Stopping at the booth to pay the attendant, circling upwards to find a spot in the structure, passing through the automatic doors, saying hello to the compassionate staff at the front desk before obtaining a parent pass. This first time it was all new, and I had no idea how many times it would be repeated. I suppose I would have been overcome with horror, unable to go on, if the length of our stay there and the depth of our suffering had been revealed to me at that moment. Thankfully, the Lord only reveals what we are able to handle. Like manna from heaven, we are given the graces we need a day at a time. So, not knowing what lie ahead, I eagerly made the trip up to see my daughter during what I was sure would be the first of only a handful of hospital visits.

The first thing one notices is the quiet. One would expect a room full of babies to be noisy. Teeming with new life, a room with eight or nine infants should be filled with the din of crying, the beautiful sounds of newborn tears. Instead, there is stillness. In the most highly-staffed rooms of the NICU, where the sickest babies are cared for, there is very little crying. Those whose breathing is assisted with ventilators cannot cry. Many are sedated to diminish their suffering. The stillness, so unnatural, is unexpected, and harsh, and unrelenting.

The next thing one realizes is that it is dark. Night or day, these rooms are kept dark. Frequently, shades are drawn, sometimes to provide the darkness conducive to restfulness, at other times to create a better environment for a procedure like an ultrasound or echocardiogram. On those rare occasions when the room is brightly lit, visitors will most likely be asked to wait outside: there is an "O.R." going on. An "operating room." A child is enduring a "procedure." A baby is receiving a treatment that would normally be done in the OR, but because it would be dangerous to move him, it is being done at the bedside. And so the room is illuminated like at no other time. It is ironic that people can be conditioned to see light as a good thing, a hopeful thing, and yet in this case a parent sees light and is immediately concerned because she knows that a precious little child is undergoing a procedure.

Everyone knows hospitals are filled with machinery, but the first time you see it all, it is completely overwhelming. There are monitors for everything; heart rate, breathing, levels of oxygen in the blood. There are plenty of tubes, wires and tape, lots of tape. And somewhere in the midst of all this technology there is your baby.

And there was my baby, my Celeste. My husband and my sister-in-law Michele, who works at the hospital as an x-ray technician, were there. There was lots of smiling, lots of laughter, as they tried to make this first visit, this reunion, seem like the easiest thing in the world. It was not. I was trembling with anticipation and fear, overcome with longing for my daughter, afraid to touch her, afraid I would harm her, afraid of the wires, afraid I would disconnect something important. I didn't even feel like she was mine. She looked so unfamiliar, like someone else's child. I do not have sickly children! I have strapping 10 pounders who cry lustily and nurse eagerly. I had produced six perfect specimens, thank you very much. This was too unreal.

But it *was* real. This was my baby, my Celeste. And although I was afraid, I reached out for her, realizing she was not that unlike my other children. As I held her I remembered the getting-to-know process. Mothers love their babies, indeed. But the honest ones will tell you it is not immediate. This child we carried within is a stranger. The fantasy child is gone, the real child here to take her place. For Celeste and me, this process had been delayed for a few days. I took the time to draw her close, to touch her gently, to kiss her tiny head. I began to love her, to risk loving her. It is always a risk to love, and never before had I felt it so acutely. There was a choice to be made, and I made it wholeheartedly. We were in this together, mother and daughter, and there was no looking back. I took the risk. I would find out later, from the nurses and chaplains who cared for us, that not all parents were willing to take that risk. It is always hard to love, to love well, and this was a place where love was tested. And so the test began.

I went home that night without her, of course. It was an amputation. A part of me, a part I could not live without, was left down the long hallway, behind the double doors. It was like leaving my very heart behind. She was being guarded by strangers, nurses who appeared competent, but strangers nonetheless. Instead of the capture of mother's loving gaze, was she held only in the care of those austere black-and-white doctors? No. I could not accept that I was leaving my baby alone, motherless. I recalled that Jesus had given me His own mother at the foot of the cross. *"Then He said to the disciple, 'Here is your mother.'"* Jesus spoke not only to John, but to me, and to Celeste. I left

Celeste in Mary's care, knowing that she was a far better mother than I could ever hope to be. She would not abandon my baby, even as I knew I must, in body if not in spirit.

Web of Prayer

*"We cannot live only for ourselves. A thousand
fibers connect us with our fellow men."*
Herman Melville

The Internet is an amazing tool. Capable of sending messages worldwide in the blink of an eye, this modern marvel is so revolutionary as to be almost incomprehensible. Email makes possible communication that just a few years ago would have been impractical. When prodded, most of us would send the occasional letter of thanks or congratulations. A wedding card, a birthday greeting.

While those archaic methods of communication still exist, most of us admit that email is the preferred mode of contacting friends and family. It wouldn't be appropriate to send out old-fashioned "snail mail'" in the way that we send out email messages each day. Because of the ease of this new method, we are overwhelmed with messages each day, so many of them useless.

We send out nonsense, much of it to people we would seldom speak to otherwise. We've all received countless jokes and stories, urban legends, and even prayer chains promising all our wishes will come true. Our fingers are usually hovering over the delete key while we check to see if there is any real substance in our inbox. Once in awhile we receive a prayer request, especially if we have managed to land ourselves a spot in the address book of a Christian friend who is also computer savvy. I had secured such a spot in several hard drives, and I knew this was time to cash in.

Celeste needed prayer, and if I could not be at her bedside 24 hours a day, if I could not hold her and nurse her and tend to her as I felt I should, as I longed to do, I would provide what she needed more than her mother. I would get those prayers.

I suppose this is a good time to reveal that since childhood, I have had a love affair with words. I had a multitude of childhood dreams, and many of them had come true. Meeting a wonderful man, having a house full of children, and learning about the beauty of the world, especially through art and theater, philosophy and religion, were lifelong dreams I had realized. But my most tender dream, the one held deepest in my heart, was to become what I *was:* a writer. I had dabbled in producing bits of material over the years, small pieces of my soul. Essays, mostly, about family life, home schooling, and faith. Pithy poems I shared with no one. Funny letters at Christmastime. Others encouraged me to spend more time writing, to seek publication, but the challenges of raising my family came first. But of course the gift was locked away with love. Like most things we cherish, it was something I was good at. It was easy for me. So that first night after I had met Celeste, I did what seemed easiest. I wrote about her.

Hello everyone,

First of all, thank you so much for your prayers for our new daughter! She is getting more beautiful each day and we are already feeling so blessed having her in our life. I know some of you may have heard some info from Chris, so forgive me if this is redundant.

Celeste is healthy and perfectly formed in most ways, but she does have a rare heart defect called Ebstein's Anomaly (which is a malformation of a heart valve) and two holes in her heart. She is also possibly battling an intestinal problem. She is not in immediate danger but it is very scary for us. What the doctors are telling us is "wait and see" which we are hearing as "wait and PRAY!" We are hoping you will all join us in doing that for Celeste.

We know that prayer is powerful, and we are asking for your help. We would love to have Celeste home for Easter. Since that is nine days from now, we are asking for a novena for her. Please pray specifically that:
**Celeste's blood oxygen levels increase
**She can safely be taken off the prostaglandin
**There is nothing wrong with her intestines
**That she may receive as complete a healing of her heart as God wills
**That she may be protected from infections
**That she can begin eating Monday so I can bring her home soon!

Celeste Marie means "heavenly Mary". She was named for our Blessed Mother, and we know Mary is looking out for us. If you can offer your rosaries for Celeste we know that will help! We are also asking for the intercession of Fr. Solanus Casey. We "thank God ahead of time" for healing our Celeste. I can't wait to tell the doctors that Celeste's improvement was the result of YOUR prayers. "God Who is mighty has done great things, and Holy is His Name!" I know there is a reason that has been going through my head since my labor began. God is already doing great things with Celeste's life. We will keep you posted.

Thank you and God Bless You
Cathy and Aaron

As I pressed "send" I realized I was taking another risk. I was asking for prayers, yes. Sounds innocent enough, but I knew that not everyone on my mailing list shared my belief in the power of prayer. I also felt deeply that this was an opportunity, an opportunity to share those beliefs and to ask for others to care for me spiritually.

It seemed important to ask for specific intentions. I remembered hearing there was power in praying this way, and as my fellow Detroiter Fr. Casey said, I should have a positive attitude. I didn't care much if I sounded overconfident or zealous. I knew Celeste needed those prayers, and I was willing to risk sounding like a "holy roller." Something told me to share this experience, that doing so was important. So I did.

A Day at the Park

"Courage is being scared to death – but saddling up anyway."
John Wayne

When a woman gives birth, but, through death or illness, is deprived of her baby's presence, it is not uncommon for her to experience physical pain. Soon I found that I was consumed by a persistent ache. Not only did my heart ache with the need to be with my daughter, but I found that my arms ached, too! They felt so heavy I could barely lift them. They should have been weary from lugging a newborn. Instead, they hurt with a profound pain, the pain of separation.

Our days soon began to form a pattern. Visiting Celeste was our priority, but we had six other children, five of them at home. The addition of another child, no matter how special, did not diminish the needs of the others. We were torn between our desire to be with the baby and the very real importance of maintaining some kind of normalcy at home. We tried to keep regular mealtimes and bedtimes. I took advantage of friends' offers to have the little boys over for playdates while I was at the hospital, so they wouldn't be as concerned by my absence. The boys and I developed a routine that involved them asking me each time I left, "When will you be home?" I would always answer, "in a couple hours" and although they had no idea how long this was, it gave them an understanding that I would return to them soon. Sometimes I took them with me to the hospital, where after a short visit with their sister they could play at "Jack's Tree House," a center for the siblings of patients.

I left the older children with simple lesson plans and chore assignments each day, so that as much as possible they were having "normal" days. I also made sure rides were available when they needed to get to some activity, and I allowed them to spend time with their friends as much as possible. Of course they wanted to spend time with their baby sister, too, so I often took one of them with me to see her. Since only two people at a time were allowed by her bedside, this gave me one-on-one time with them, something I know was important to them, and me.

While we did our best to maintain as typical a home life as possible for our family, Aaron and I began what even the NICU doctors called "The Roller Coaster Ride." When Celeste was having a good day, so were we. When she wasn't, the descent began. This was no amusement park, though. Those weary arms were not bravely waving over our heads, they were clutching the safety bar tightly, knuckles white.

So we visited. Talked to endless doctors. Came home and did laundry. Ate meals prepared for us by friends. Prayed. And sent emails.

Aaron wrote this.

> Today's update is that Celeste had a couple tests done on the intestines and they all came back negative!! No problems at this time. The doctors are to discuss another precautionary test but please pray they decide it's not necessary, as they would have to put Celeste under general anesthesia.

The echocardiogram on her heart came back looking the same as before. So they tell us we are still in a wait and pray status. They don't want to move too quickly.

Best news of the day is that she can now eat!!! Cathy and I both had the opportunity to feed her with a bottle, although they have her on a limited amount. I pray this is the beginning of the process of bringing her HOME.

Please keep praying on Celeste's behalf and thank you for all your prayers thus far.

Then I took over.

First of all thank you again for keeping us all in your prayers! Celeste is still in the hospital but she has made some progress. The intestinal issues that the doctors were investigating have been resolved. As Mom thought all along, she is fine in that department. They ended up doing a biopsy on her colon, which turned out ok. Unfortunately the antibiotic that she was on for her first week may have given her some problems. Starting last Tuesday she went into kidney failure. All the docs were puzzled as to why it was happening (they should have listened to Mom again!) but they finally figured it was a drug reaction. This was most distressing to us because a drug she never needed to be on caused it! But the good news is her blood tests show she is improving and her kidneys look fine on ultrasound and she is peeing well! We are also happy to report she is eating well and even nursing with Mom!

The next hurdle is getting her off the prostaglandin. Hopefully they will try to do that today. Please pray that her blood oxygen levels stay in the 80s and they will send her home. It is such a cross for the whole family not having her home with us.

Mom also needs some extra prayers. I must admit I have my moments when I don't think I can take another minute of this! My blood pressure (which was high for the last part of my pregnancy) has also continued to increase and my doc put me on meds for it. I know I need to keep it together for the family so I humbly ask you to send up an extra prayer for me too!

Your prayers are so precious to us. We don't know how we could get through this without the support of our friends, family, parish family and home school community. We love and appreciate you all.

I just took a moment to read the email I sent to you all a while back, and I am happy to report that many of our prayers are being answered! God is so good to us!

A Day at the Park

Celeste continues to improve. Two days ago they stopped the prostaglandins, and she is doing quite well. The ductus in her heart is still open (that was the effect of the prostaglandin) so we are keeping our fingers crossed that when it closes she will still have good oxygen saturation of her blood. Please pray specifically for that.

Her kidneys are getting better as well. Unfortunately she still has a lot of edema around her eyes because of that, but she is getting better each day. She is up to 7lbs 9oz and looking chubby like our other kids.

Mom is hanging in there. Thank you for praying for me too. I couldn't do it without you all and my wonderful husband who is doing his best to keep things going around here.

Thank you for your continued prayers.

Prayers requested. Prayers answered. All the while adding to our vocabularies, expanding our medical knowledge more than we ever dreamed. While Mom and Dad rode the coaster, Celeste jumped on the "medical merry-go-round." One drug led to another, one procedure to the next. We quickly learned that doctors were trained to assume the worst when any new symptom presented. Since her tummy was slightly distended, the doctors feared she might have Hirschsprungs Disease, and ordered an intestinal biopsy. This led to a routine course of antibiotics. The antibiotics led to kidney failure. The results came back, no Hirschsrungs, kidneys ok. For now, she was passing each test. Biopsies, heart echoes, ultrasounds. Blood tests, so many blood tests, some days almost hourly. Her tiny fingers and toes were covered with marks. I remembered when my other children required even one such blood draw, and how upset I had become. Now my Celeste was being poked and prodded, being tested beyond my comprehension, but I told myself it was a necessary evil, part of the required path that would soon bring her home to me. Just making it through each day felt like a test, but as I left her each night I was still certain our separation would be brief. We were at the top of the hill. Can you hear the "click, click, click" on the tracks? Hold on tight. You know what's coming next.

Sorrow Shared

"If a friend of mine... gave a feast, and did not invite me to it, I should not mind a bit...But if a friend of mine had a sorrow and refused to allow me to share it, I would feel it most bitterly...he who can look on the loveliness of the world and share its sorrow, and realize something of the wonder of both, is in immediate contact with divine things, and has got as near to God's secret as anyone can get."
Oscar Wilde

On the evening of April 5, the coaster went careening down a mighty big hill. When that day's thrill ride was over, I fled the darkness of the NICU, drove home through the black night, and entered a new darkness in my soul. For the first time, the question was no longer hypothetical. *Would my daughter die tonight?*

To say that Aaron and I were traumatized by what happened that night would be a gross understatement. We arrived at the NICU that day expecting more of the same. More waiting, more questions for the doctors and attending nurses. More hope that she would be home soon. Instead we held her in our arms and tried to feed her a bottle, and watched something go very wrong.

When the nurses said she had a rough day, we thought it nothing more than a day of fussiness. Isn't that what a "rough day" was for an infant? A few extra minutes settling in for a nap. Maybe a bit of colic. But I could not compare Celeste to my other children, so even though I was an experienced mother I can't say I knew at first that anything was really wrong. When her nurse reported that she had fussed all day, finally calming down when a guitarist from music therapy came to play for her, I assumed she was just being a normal baby.

When I noticed she was turning pale and starting to perspire, I began to do the same.

Something was really wrong here.

Aaron was holding her, trying to feed her a bottle, when she began to gasp. They had told us that babies with cardiac conditions often had trouble feeding, that sometimes it was just too much work for them. We told the nurse of our concerns, and the stillness of the nursery began to change dramatically. A technician took a blood sample and made a grim announcement: She was "acidotic." This meant, ultimately, that she was not getting enough oxygen. "Bag her!" the nurse shouted, and I stood at her bedside, essentially helpless, while they applied an oxygen mask to her face. It wasn't working. "We need to intubate her NOW!" For a moment everything took on a surreal quality. It was one of those moments when life seems like a movie. I had a starring role as the mother of the baby in crisis, and it was terrifying. I offered up a quick prayer, and immediately felt a maternal presence. Mary was with me, in a very real way. I asked her to take care of my baby. With that we were quickly ushered out while they prepared to put Celeste on a ventilator.

We wept in the hall outside her room, convinced

we would never see her alive again. Somehow we made our way to the waiting room, trembling, overcome with concern. Almost immediately a nurse appeared, bringing with her a tall black woman, Rosalind, whom she introduced as one of the chaplains. I began to swoon. I knew it meant Celeste had died.

Quickly, the nurse assured me that the doctors were taking care of Celeste, doing everything they needed to do. The chaplain was there to pray with us, if we desired.

The sight of Rosalind, calm and commanding, was a comfort. I could tell that she had done this many times before. Like a mother hen, she gathered Aaron and me to her and put her arms around us. Her words were balm: "Would you like to pray?"

I don't remember her exact words, but I do recall feeling a powerful healing presence as she spoke. Her faith tradition was different from ours, but at that moment we were simply brethren. Human beings who cared about one another. It was not the first time a believer of another faith had prayed for us, nor would it be the last. I was infinitely grateful for the gifts her church had given her, especially her knowledge of scripture and her ability to allow the Spirit to lead her prayers. As we talked, I continued to weep. She asked if we were believers. We nodded, and she had another question. "Do you trust Him?" I nodded again. "Then why are you crying?"

It was said with such kindness; not a trace of harshness or judgment entered her tone. Why indeed. If I trusted God to do only the best for Celeste, then I should not cry. But my human heart was afraid. I was only a mother, after all. I knew Rosalind was right, though, and I dried my tears. It was time to let go of Celeste, to really give in to that faith in my Lord.

The next day was the first day I did not visit Celeste. I stayed home and took care of my other children, and allowed others to care for me. I gave the nurses permission to stand in my place. I knew that she would be well cared for, and that my trust lay not in human skill but in the love of my heavenly father. I shared my sorrow with the following email:

> Celeste has had quite a setback. Last night she was having a lot of difficulty breathing. We were both with her -- thank God Aaron was paying close attention to her! The nurse said she had been "fussy" all day but it turned out to be more than that. She is now in acute care again and on a ventilator and lots of medicine. Her condition is quite serious-- a lung problem called pulmonary hypertension.
>
> We know so many people are praying for her. We know God is in control. But we are very

frightened. We are trying to accept God's will for her whatever it may be, but we really need your continued prayer support. Last night was the worst thing we have ever experienced. The suffering we are feeling is so intense. Please pray for us.

We know that God has a plan for Celeste's life, and that His will is perfect. We know that she will glorify Him in a unique way, and that "all things work together for the good of those who love Him." Despite all our pain we are so happy to have our Celeste.

I was not by her side, but I prayed continually. Breathing in and out became a form of prayer. I looked at the crucifix that hung in my home, gaining a fresh perspective. This cross, the one *I* carried, would lead to a secret path into His heart, truly a path to real happiness. I did not suffer alone. I contemplated the ancient image with new eyes. There was a reason the back of the cross was bare: that spot was reserved for me.

Whole-hearted Love

*"Wheresoever you go,
go there with your whole heart."*
Confucius

Every day began with a recommitment of my love and dedication to Celeste. I understood how very much this reflected our life with Christ. Every day is an opportunity to rededicate ourselves, to continue building a relationship that He established on the cross. And so it was with my darling daughter. Each day was a new opportunity to show her my love.

It was so difficult to see her like this. The nurses were gentle as they explained the functions and settings on her ventilator, the doctors matter-of-fact while they confessed they did not know the precise reason for her decline.

She laid perfectly still, her tiny, pale body very bloated. She was heavily sedated: I wished I were. At times we admitted we wanted to run. It was just too awful, the pain was too intense. I looked at her lying there and realized that largely what I was feeling was disappointment. Profound, gripping, honest to goodness disappointment.

When you have had four boys in succession, the birth of a girl seems like an impossible dream. The ultrasound I had at 18 weeks was inconclusive, but we were fairly certain we were having a little girl, and we were over the moon. As soon as the ultrasound tech confirmed that no male parts were clearly visible, I began to see pink. Pink sleepers, pink hair bows, pink blankets, pink dresses. Oh, the pink dresses. I began to shop early in my pregnancy, hoping I was indeed having that girl. When a friend offered to throw a shower, I have to say it, I was tickled PINK! It is a bad pun, but a truly apt description of how I felt. I joked that I was drowning in a sea of pink. I was thrilled.

Now my baby girl was here, and there were no

pink dresses. She was dressed only in a diaper, a diaper that most frequently was changed by others. I could not bathe her and brush her wispy hair. I could not take her to church and show her off to the little old ladies who had been awaiting her birth. I began to feel no small measure of guilt about this disappointment. Shouldn't I be more "spiritual" than this? Shouldn't I be only concerned about her welfare, not pouting because the fun I was anticipating was being denied? But truly, I was disappointed, and angry. This was most definitely not what I had planned.

On April 10 I sent out an update to our friends. It was the morning of Celeste's baptism day, and I was making an effort to see the joy in this. I prepared her gown, the same one worn by me and my other two daughters. I would not be able to dress her in it; it simply laid on top of her very still little body.

> I'm sorry it's taken a few days for this update. After the last one I know you were all concerned about Celeste.
>
> There is some good news! Celeste is doing much better. It turns out she has pneumonia, which is being treated with antibiotics. Apparently that triggered the episode the other night. The diagnosis of pulmonary hypertension is a bit confusing to me. The doctors call it "primary"

which means it is unrelated to her heart condition. But they are treating it appropriately. Aaron emailed an expert in Colorado and amazingly he responded right away. He confirmed they were treating her properly (and the doctor at Children's said he knew him). Anyway, the important thing is she is responding to the treatment. Our doctor said if she didn't respond well the prognosis was not good, so we are thrilled she appears to be doing so well. She is still on the respirator and lots of meds but her nurse said yesterday they are weaning her off everything and she is doing well. After we get through this setback we will need to find out what is next for her heart, but we are taking it one day at a time.

She is still sedated but yesterday she was much more reactive. She likes to put her right hand to her cheek to comfort herself and she was doing that. She was wiggling her little toes and smiling in her sleep. It was so nice to be able to smile at her bedside!

Today we are filled with joy, as Fr. Jeff will be coming to the hospital to baptize her. (We know the Aquafina Aaron used when she was one day old did the trick, but we thought we'd make it official.)

I want you all to know that I have been praying for you all, too. I know it is hard to take this journey with us and to keep praying when you hear sad news. But I have been thanking God for you every day and asking him to bless you for the love you are showing us. Please don't get discouraged.

> Sometimes it seems God is not listening when he doesn't answer the way we'd like, or answer fast enough. But as my very wise brother keeps reminding me, prayer doesn't change God, it changes us. It may very well be that it's not Celeste's heart that needs to be repaired. It may be our hearts that need to change.

So on the morning of the 8th, and every day thereafter, when I entered the darkness of the NICU, when I saw Celeste lying there in bed A-1, the bed reserved in this acute care room for the sickest babies, I tried to sweep aside this profound disappointment. I knew that I did not have my fantasy baby; I had Celeste. I did not, of course, know how long I would have her, but I became profoundly aware that there are no guarantees for any of us. I realized that *I* might not even make it home alive. Each day -- for each of us-- is a gift. I decided that I would look at each day with Celeste as the gift that it was. I did not ever want to look back on any time in her life with bitterness. This note went out to friends on April 18. On the subject line I wrote "Lessons from Celeste."

> Here's some news about our dear Celeste. They were able to take her off the respirator last Wednesday, and she has continued to recover since then. She is in an intermediate room now and looking more like her old self. She is still on

oxygen and some medication but she is much, much better. We were able to begin bottle-feeding her a small amount again, and today I was even able to give her a bath! What a joy to be able to hold her again! The nurses who cared for her when she was so sick are amazed at the speed of her recovery from the pneumonia. I am not surprised because I know so many people are praying for her! Aaron and I are convinced that the whole world is praying for us — what a great feeling. She is on international prayer lists, folks in Poland are praying, whole churches of various denominations are praying for her. I know many old friends have been asking about her and I am so touched at your concern. Thank you again.

I referred to lessons in this email because it seems Celeste is teaching me something every day and I wanted to share it with you. A few days after she got so ill I was feeling so sad at all the things I have missed with her -- not being able to hold her, dress her, take her home, etc. But I realized I have to accept her as she is each day, to really love her unconditionally. I realized I wanted her to do things for me, to make me happy by being a healthy little baby like all my other children. But she taught me that she deserves my love just because she is. I have to take each day with her as the absolute blessing that it is. We all need to do that with all our loved ones every day! So thank God right now for your family, for your children. Thank Him whether or not they are healthy. He has blessed each of us so much!

Tomorrow the doctors will be consulting about what sort of options we have about Celeste's heart. Please pray that if surgery is necessary the outcome is good. And when you pray for our family, please also remember the other families of kids at Children's. There is so much suffering there.

It was humbling to learn such an important lesson from a tiny baby, but I began that day to realize that she was an excellent teacher.

First Fruits

*"Act as if what you do makes a difference.
It does."*
William James

As our requests for support spread out through the web, prayers rained down upon us. Daily we received emails confirming that our need was being shared with many. It is difficult to describe the true nature of prayer, impossible to say just how this attempt on the part of mere creatures to converse with their God can impact us. In our case, the prayers of others became an invisible net that sustained us. These prayers were real, not just wishes or thoughts, but incredible tools with the power to transform.

It became clear that Celeste was touching many lives. Members of our parish and the homeschool community to which we belonged prayed faithfully and offered meals and conversation. A friend in our church family, whom I've known since high school, made sure I heard from classmates living around the country. Co-workers of my husband's shared Celeste's needs with friends and family, and a network of prayer support developed throughout our community. Relatives in Poland prayed, including a cousin of Aaron's, a priest who asked his congregation to remember Celeste. Churches of various denominations put her on prayer lists. Several orders of nuns in different locales interceded for her. At one point I heard that the Mother Superior in a cloistered order read my email updates to the sisters as they ate their evening meal.

People who didn't pray prayed for Celeste. There is something about a tiny baby in need that can make miracles like that happen.

One morning I was visiting Celeste when a woman I had never seen before entered her room. She identified herself as a doctor -- a dentist, in fact -- who worked downstairs. *A dentist*, I thought, *how odd!*

Celeste didn't even have any teeth! Then she revealed the reason for her visit. She was receiving my emails and wanted to meet the child for whom she had been praying. I was amazed and heartened.

Hospital staff had introduced me to several mothers of children who had undergone heart surgery. I was attracted at once to the mother of a little boy, age six, who had a heart transplant as an infant. Due to her gentle demeanor and kind spirit, I was not surprised to discover she was a Christian. It *was* surprising to discover she had been praying for me before we met — her husband belonged to a work-related prayer group and had been receiving my emails and sharing them. Amazing.

It is impossible to overestimate the impact of each confirmation I received that Celeste's intentions were not being forgotten. I ran to my computer each day, hoping for notes. I saved each one, treasuring the fact that Celeste was being prayed for, treasuring the fact that no matter what happened, Celeste's life was touching people. The messages showered me with wisdom and solace and joy.

From a high school friend: *"It seems like I worry about such little things regarding my children that can't even compare to the severity of Celeste's problems. Your letters help me to keep things in perspective and to know that my family has been blessed tremendously. God has a purpose for each trial we face..."*

From a friend whose own child died tragically at the age of two: *"We are like a child in need begging for our Father's attention and comfort. We want Him to fix it now and it's hard for us to understand why He's not doing it. I compare it to a little one needing to nurse. All they understand is that they are uncomfortably hungry and they want to eat! They can't understand that we will be home in 15 minutes and they can snuggle and get a drink then. So we try to comfort them with soothing words in a gentle voice, while the child cries, until we can finally get home to give them what they want. We are that hungry child. We can't understand why God's not fixing it-- we are begging! But, the Almighty, all Powerful, all Knowing all LOVING God can see that "we'll be home in 15 minutes" and although it's painful He's still there."*

From the sister of Aaron's coworker, whom we had never met, writing to a long list of friends from her church: *"Please pray for Celeste...I can feel the heartbreak they are experiencing...please pray that God will wrap His arms around them, giving them comfort and reassurance....Pray that God will continue to guide the doctors and nurses that care for this precious child that is loved by so many. Pray that through each and every day, the people (who) are able to help this family will find ways and will continue to reach out as an extension of God's love. Please pray that Cathy and Aaron will remember that in receiving help from others, they are in fact being a blessing to (those who) reach out."*

"*Please find encouragement that when you just can't do it anymore, there is still someone praying.*" This note came from a woman we've not met to this day. One lady, a friend of my mother's, forwarded our messages to friends in Atlanta and California. A man at church we didn't know very well wrote "*your family has touched so many lives....Celeste has really had an impact on me...I think about her 24/7.*"

I was happy that God was using us to touch others. More than once I used the emails to share my thoughts on faith and how grace was working in our lives.

> I'd like to share something I realized today, if you don't mind me "preaching" again! I was thinking about how unfair it seems that Celeste has had to suffer so many setbacks. If we are all praying so much, why does God allow this? It occurred to me that it is similar to our spiritual lives. Some of us

have committed serious sins and God has saved us from them, helping us to repent. Others have never really fallen into serious sin, not because they are "holier" but because God prevented their fall. In Celeste's case, he can protect her from challenges or allow them to occur and then show His power by saving her from them. See what I mean? Both ways show His power -- it's just up to Him to determine which way will be for His greater glory. The challenge for me is to remember to let God be God!

Like a pebble in a pond, little Celeste's life was sending ripples into the world.

A New Heart

"Perseverance is impossible if we don't permit ourselves to hope."
Dean Koontz' Odd Thomas

"A parent's worst nightmare." How many times have we heard that phrase? It seems that every article I've ever read, every made-for-TV movie I've ever seen in which parents discover their child is ill, features the phrase. As Celeste's life advanced those words took on a sublime personal meaning. Is it a nightmare the day you find out your baby isn't perfectly healthy? Is it a nightmare when you find out your child needs surgery?

Does the bad dream continue when you realize your child might die? Or is the only true horror when you lose all hope your child will live, and death becomes a certainty?

Our days in the NICU took on a dreamlike quality, to be sure. But we had decided we could not bear to describe it as a nightmare. We were experiencing our daughter's life, and we chose to boldly walk with faith, with joy in the small moments.

Some days this was quite difficult to do.

There is nothing so surreal as the moment they tell you your child needs a heart transplant, barring perhaps the moment that you wait in a conference room to talk to the nurse in charge of the program and realize there are several picnic coolers sitting around the room. Could it be that they actually use these vessels to transport human organs? As Aaron and I waited to meet Joanne we laughed nervously and told each other they were most likely there to keep drinks cold. Of course we were wrong.

What a strange room. The large conference table in the center was surrounded by shelves of large books, their binders featuring the names of every heart defect known to man. We spotted the one Celeste had -- Ebstein's anomaly -- and discovered what percentage of infants with the defect don't survive. I don't recall the number. I was too chilled by the whole experience. What were we doing here? How could it be possible that we even had to consider such a thing? Could we really be here to discuss our daughter receiving the heart of another child? Could it be possible that this was her only hope?

I discovered with a growing certainty that Celeste's defect was quite severe, and I had come to accept that she would certainly require surgery someday. But when the doctors suggested that she may need a transplant, I was shaken. *A heart transplant.* What would have to happen for a transplant to occur was more than I could comprehend. What mother wants to play the scene out in her mind: another precious child would have to die. His or her healthy heart would be removed, and my daughter's chest would be cut open to receive it, her diseased organ, the one that God had given her, tossed aside. It seemed so ghastly. We were overwhelmed and afraid.

The doctors assured us all parents felt that way. They were professional beyond measure, and much more gentle than I would've imagined. They had us meet with the nurse in charge of the program to discuss any questions we may have, and I prepared myself, as best as humanly possible, for what might be coming next.

Joanne turned out to be quite the opposite of what I feared. She immediately put us at ease with her kind smile and gentle demeanor. I was taken with her Canadian accent and the way she referred to the children she cared for as "kiddos." I felt we were kindred spirits, especially when she expressed her belief that each person has a unique purpose, that each life was important regardless of the length of days it lasted. I could tell that although we most likely had differences in the expressions of our spirituality, we had much in common.

She was indeed kind, but also straightforward. It seemed that candor was becoming critical to our dealing with this situation. She assured us that she would be there for us every step of the way, but emphasized that a heart transplant was not a cure. She said some families thought you got a new organ, and a pat on the back, and were sent on your merry way. The reality was much more complex. It was during times like that in which fear wanted to take hold of me; during those times where even the best news brought the reality of the depth of Celeste's condition.

Aaron and I were now filled with new questions. Our first concern was about the ethical nature of organ transplants. Although the doctors had assured us that transplants were morally acceptable by all major religions, we were concerned. I had heard that organs were taken from people who were not yet dead, and I knew this was wrong. Could we even consider a transplant for our daughter?

After meeting with Joanne to learn the medical facts of a transplant, we knew the first thing we needed to do was address these moral concerns. I had a friend contact moral theologian and seminary professor Mark Latkovic. We were relieved to hear the church did allow organ transplants, but considered them "extraordinary means" of care that families did not have to accept. Dr. Latkovic noted that the organ donor must indeed be dead before the organs were harvested, and explained that there was some controversy about when death actually occurred. We spent much time discussing what this meant in our situation. Since it would be impossible for us to actually verify this for ourselves in our particular situation, it became clear that we would have to trust the surgeons to follow correct procedures. The moral culpability lay on them, not us.

This was difficult for me to accept, and yet I had to confidently accept this realization so that we could move forward. I lived my life by my Catholic faith, and I was committed to following the teachings of my church. More than anything, I wanted to do the right thing. Aaron and I prayed about how best to do this. We wanted life for Celeste, but we did not want to do anything immoral. After much soul-searching we decided we would pursue the option of the transplant, knowing we would never judge a family who might make a different decision. We prayed the same respect would be afforded to us.

We realized that although a tremendous amount of people were praying for Celeste, most of them did not realize how severe her defect was. On April 23 we sent out this note:

> Just a note to update you once again. Celeste has had a bit of a setback. She is back in acute care because she began having trouble breathing on Thursday. She has congestion in her lung and her blood pressure is up. She's now in an oxygen tent and doing a bit better.
>
> Of course we are disappointed because just a few days ago they were talking about sending her home soon. But it looks like her heart is not doing as well as we hoped with medical therapy. The docs consulted about her and basically came up with two paths she may take. If she responds to the medical therapy and doesn't have any more setbacks, she could possibly hang in there until she would need surgery on her valve as a teenager. The other option is a heart transplant. There seems to be nothing in between these two extremes. We visited with the transplant nurse to begin

understanding what may be necessary for Celeste. How surreal it all is! We know many of you are probably shocked to hear this may be what Celeste needs. We know that many people did not realize how severe her heart defect is. But we are starting to prepare for this possibility, which is more likely now that she is not doing well once again.

I almost feel silly asking for your prayers again. I know that you are all praying. Sometimes we feel such an outpouring of grace, such extraordinary peace in the midst of our suffering that we know your prayers are holding us up. Other than Celeste's condition, I will extend another prayer request. Pray that we may be able to better handle balancing the needs of our family. It has been so challenging to take care of everyone's needs, manage the house, etc.

Thank you for caring about us. We so appreciate your love and support.

We knew that the idea of a heart transplant was truly unfathomable to most people. Most, myself included, did not know much about the procedure, the risks, and the likelihood of success. As I became educated, I shared what I learned.

I have been thinking about her heart transplant (of course) and I thought I'd share some of the things we've learned. First of all, the surgery itself is not the riskiest heart surgery there is. In fact, the survival rate is something like 97%. The first six months after surgery are intense, but after that, if all goes well, the survival rates are also excellent. As the years go by the rates begin dropping, in large part because of non-compliance with medication. Celeste will be on meds for immune system suppression permanently. The docs say they have a huge problem getting teenagers to continue taking their meds, so the mortality rate is affected by this. At first she will be taking 40-50 doses a day of 10-12 meds. After one year she will probably be down to 2 meds.

Rejection of the organ is common, in fact it is to be expected. It's not like in the movies when they say with surprise "She's rejecting the organ!" The degree of rejection can vary greatly, and treatment involves manipulating all those meds. The younger they are when they receive the heart the better-- less rejection occurs before the age of three months. (Celeste is 11 weeks old today.)

Celeste will probably be in the hospital for 3-4 weeks after her surgery. The nurses keep telling us she will almost immediately be like a different baby. They say it is amazing how quickly she will recover and that the majority of babies do extremely well post-transplant.

Celeste's new heart will not last a lifetime, only about 15-20 years. Most likely she will then receive another heart, but who knows what kind of advances will occur in that time! We cannot worry about 20 years from now!

Also, it is true that nationwide 25-30% of the infants waiting for a heart die while waiting. But the good news is that in the seven years that they have been doing transplants at Children's, they have never had a baby die waiting for a heart. You can be sure I cling to this fact when I fear her heart will never come. Celeste will be unique as she will be the first baby with Ebstein's anomaly to receive a transplant at Children's. Usually the condition is not severe enough to require a transplant and other surgeries are an effective treatment.

The waiting time for a heart for an infant can be several months, not the years that adults wait. This is because the demand for infant hearts is not as great. The longest wait for an infant heart at Children's was about three months. Celeste's wait theoretically will be shorter because she is 1-A, the highest priority for a transplant.

The bottom line is that the prognosis for Celeste is quite good. Once she receives her heart and makes it through those first six months or so, she will be pretty much like most other kids. She will have a suppressed immune system and will have to avoid some situations (swimming in certain lakes, playing in sandboxes, owning birds as pets) but in most ways she will be very ordinary! How extraordinary that will be!

I was anxious, afraid, and overwhelmed. But I was also filled with hope. They had given us hope.

Suffering

"If there is a meaning in life at all, then there must be a meaning in suffering. Suffering is an ineradicable part of life, even as fate and death. Without suffering and death human life cannot be complete."
Viktor Frankl, "Man's Search for Meaning"

very time someone sends me a note I cry, sometimes just feeling relieved that someone is thinking about us and praying for us. I am just so tired of waiting!

Sometimes I just dive into all the reasons I have to suffer. It's such a long litany. I remember the feeling when the transport team took her the night she was born. I recall how I felt driving home from the hospital without her, going into our house and seeing the other kids and the "It's a girl" sign, but without a baby. The times I've called the hospital and they said she had a bad night. The time her heart rate dropped into the 50s and they had to massage it back to life. Or the time they had to shock it back into a proper rhythm. Neither time, was I with her. Where was I, her mother, when she was suffering? I wasn't there when she had her spinal tap, either. It's just not right. My arms ache for her every day, and my heart feels like it's living outside my body. And then I just thank God she is even alive, and that we have hope.

It's funny though, one of my biggest pain inducers is thinking about clothes! This little Easter outfit she never wore, the sleepers that were returned for a larger size, the summer dresses I bought last year on clearance just keeping my fingers crossed for a little girl. I know there are other moms who have suffered more. She is alive. There is hope. But some days it feels like she will never come home. And I just want her here so badly. Every holiday that passes just brings on more pain. We joke that maybe she will be home by Christmas, but it's not funny any more.

The days in the NICU lengthened into weeks, the weeks into months. Each day we visited Celeste and cared for our family as best we could. Aaron returned

Suffering

to work; I made feeble attempts at home schooling the other children. Lauren and I shopped for a prom dress; Lukie celebrated his third birthday. We attended Lauren's graduation commencement and even hosted a party for her. Easter came and went, then Mother's Day, Memorial Day, Father's Day, the Fourth of July. Time kept going in the world around us, but in the NICU there was one constant. There was suffering.

The suffering in Celeste's life was not the whole story, but to deny it existed would be a lie. Daily, I told myself she did not suffer so much. She was in the care of trained nurses who were highly competent and even loving. She was heavily sedated much of the time. She would never remember any of this anyway, right? No big deal.

> You know it is so hard for us to see her suffer. One of the nurses was reassuring me that Celeste will never remember any of this (which of course I know) because one of her drugs causes amnesia. But this only makes me sad because I also know she has no memory of me, either. It's like she's a little sleeping beauty there. I only wish they could put the whole castle to sleep with her, like in the fairy tale.
>
> Please pray also for Aaron and me. We are both feeling so afraid. We know that God has only His

best in store for our family, and we know His will is perfect. But our human nature just wants our dear baby. We so wanted this little girl to love, we had so many dreams for her. We are trying to hold on to those dreams but we realize God may have a different plan.

But it was a big deal. The place where Celeste's suffering is acknowledged is a place I cannot visit too frequently; the pain it evokes is too raw. But to deny the existence of it, to not realize its value and even its beauty would be wrong.

She suffered. From the moment of her birth, she was denied the comfort of her mother's arms, and the joy of nursing. She was dressed not in soft terrycloth sleepers selected with love by her sisters, but in hospital issued white t-shirts, or more commonly, only a diaper. She did not sleep in a quiet nursery with a crib set up by her big brother, but in a cold plastic unit lit by a heat lamp. Instead of spending her days in the company of her siblings, learning to smile and coo, she spent them waiting for ultrasounds and MRIs. Small sufferings? Maybe.

Some, however, were certainly more intense. She endured more IV procedures than I can remember, some involving the OR method known as a "cut-down." Her head was even partially shaved for some of these, while others were inserted into her hands, feet, chest and even her jugular vein. One of my clearest memories is of the day the IV in her neck became displaced. I had actually dressed her that day, and I will never forget the little pink Winnie-the-Pooh outfit she wore. I was holding her when I discovered the IV was coming out. My arm, her outfit, covered with blood. There is nothing like seeing your baby's blood. No drama is intended with this statement, just the truth, the very depth of what had become our baby's life.

I should have been used to the sight of blood, maybe should have become anesthetized to it, but I did not, could not, would not allow myself. Maybe in that way I was able to share in Celeste's suffering and found comfort in that. Just as Mary most assuredly suffered with her innocent Son, I, too, was suffering with my innocent daughter.

She received several blood transfusions. Her fingers and toes were constant sources of blood for tests. A ventilator tube was down her throat most of her life, a tube that had to be frequently suctioned, causing her much discomfort. A bout with RSV caused her lungs to fill with fluid. Because she was fed for a time only IV nutrition, and not the breast milk I pumped for her, she became severely jaundiced, so much so that even her tears were bright yellow. Not that she could really cry. Because of her ventilator, she could make no sounds. When she cried she merely grimaced, her face silently contorted. But I cried for her, my heart willingly ready to beat for hers.

When it was feared a yeast infection might damage her eyes, she endured, without the aid of pain-relieving medication, an exam that included metal apparatus inserted in her eyes to hold them open. A concern about meningitis led to a spinal tap. Verifying the pressures in her lungs meant she needed a heart catheterization, a procedure that is certainly uncomfortable. She was given medicines daily that caused a variety of side effects including a high temperature, irritability, vomiting, unusual hair growth, edema and a strange stiffness and swelling in her legs. She often had horrible diarrhea. The rash that came as a result was so severe that it bled continually, becoming, I'm sure, one of her most painful sufferings.

Of course as we watched her endure these trials we suffered as well. I stayed by her bedside as often as they would allow, sometimes fighting off the urge to faint. One of my greatest sufferings was that of leaving her each day. Several days before she was born, I had watched Mel Gibson's *The Passion of the Christ*. I did not know at the time I would be entering into an intense passion of my own; it was Lent, and I was preparing for Easter and what I thought would be a limited experience of pain during my child's birth. Now, as I suffered with Celeste, suffered at leaving her, I remembered scenes from the film in vivid detail. I was moved most by the images of Mary and Jesus. I recalled the scene in which Mary remembers Jesus as a child, comforting him when He fell. Now, as He walks to Cavalry, she is unable to go to Him. I remembered also the scene in which Mary is looking for Jesus on the night He was taken into custody. Since she is united so closely to Him, she knows He is present. She touches the ground, knowing He is imprisoned in a cell beneath, but once again, she cannot be with Him. On the day Celeste's blood covered my arm, I recalled the scene in which Mary wiped her Son's Precious Blood from the pavement.

  These images reminded me that I did not suffer alone. I experienced a new kinship with the mother of Jesus, who was my mother as well. I knew that she had felt as I did, tortured as she watched her innocent child suffer. I knew that she was praying for me, encouraging me to trust her son, who had endured His sufferings for Celeste and me.

  We tried daily to take these graces with us into the ICU. Watching Celeste suffer would have been enough to bear, but there was more. We witnessed the death of more than one child there. We saw other families weep with despair. We fought boredom and monotony. We ate the not always nutritious food in the hospital cafeteria (amusingly-named the "Young at Heart" Cafe.) We left our other children daily, only to feel we were abandoning Celeste when we left the hospital. We spent over a hundred nights at home waiting for the phone to ring with an announcement of bad news on the other end. There was suffering to spare -- suffering filling our cup and running over. But we continued on because we had no choice. We focused on the hope the doctors had given us, the hope that Celeste would receive a new heart and begin a new life. We trusted them and we trusted God. And still we suffered.

Through it all I had a deep sense that we were a part of something important, something bigger, as they say. I repeatedly told this to David, our social worker, who frequently visited. David was another vessel of God's mercy to us. A Catholic who happened to be a home-schooling father, his faith was a gift to us, his presence a comfort. Often he would stop by Celeste's bed and ask how we were doing. I told him the truth; we were doing very well, we were doing horribly.

Marilyn, a hospital chaplain who was especially kind to us, reminded me more than once during this time that God was in control. "Remember," she said, "all things for the good of those who love him. And I know you love Him!" But as the months passed, I became overwhelmed with everything. I remember telling David and Marilyn that it had to end soon, that this anguish couldn't last forever. We talked frequently about how true that was, and about the truth that we were indeed a part of something important. At the time I thought we were talking about the heart transplant; now I think it might have been something even bigger than what was immediately apparent.

As I reflect on Celeste's sufferings, the Lord has allowed me to see that Celeste's life, her agonies, were indeed "something big." I offered her sufferings and mine to Him in prayer, and He revealed to me the following scene.

Celeste is in Jesus' arms. It is moments before her birth, and the two of them are having a little talk.

He is telling her it is almost time for her to be born, and she is hesitant. "I don't want to leave you," she cries.

"You must go, Celeste, but don't worry, you will be back with me soon."

"Why must I go? Can't I just stay here with you? I love you so much. I don't want to go to that horrible place."

Jesus smiles. "You know they are waiting for you, Celeste. You have to spend a little time there doing some work for me."

Celeste smiles too. She wants to please Jesus, and it isn't hard because she loves him so much.

"You are right, Earth can seem a horrible place, but some of it is quite beautiful. I am giving you a very special family. You have a mother, a father and six brothers and sisters. You have aunts, uncles, cousins and grandparents. I have chosen just the right family for you. They have been prepared by me their whole lives to receive you."

"Do they love you, Jesus?" Celeste wants know.

"Oh, yes, they love me," he assures her.

Celeste smiles again. She would be sad if her family did not share her love of God.

"Then I will be happy to go to them, Jesus."

Jesus holds her close to His Heart. "I will miss you while you are gone, but we will never really be separated. You are so special to me, my little sister. I feel so close to you that I want you to be a lot like me while you are on earth. But I will not force this on you. You must choose. Do you want to do this for me?"

Celeste's smile grows even broader. She is so excited.

Jesus smiles too. He knew, of course, that she

would respond just this way.

"While you are there, you will suffer greatly. You will feel much pain, and you will be denied the comfort of your mother's arms. You will be separated from this family that loves you so much, and you will never go home to live with them.

"Like me, you will be a sign of contradiction. You will be innocent and pure but you will live a life of pain. It will be hard for some to understand, but the eyes of many will be opened by my grace, and I will use you to bring many souls to my Heart. When you return to me, we will never again be separated. I choose you, Celeste. Are you ready to go?"

Celeste holds her tiny hands over her heart and looks in the eyes of her Savior. She is overcome with peace. Jesus is asking so little of her, she thinks. He is the King of Kings, the Holy One, and He is asking her to serve him in a singular way! What an exquisite honor!

Each smiles a gentle smile. An unspoken "yes" passes between them. Jesus cradles her one last time, holding His wounded hand over his Heart. The Love contained there bursts forth like the rays of the sun, and He sends her to us, a pure and sacred gift to be briefly held, and then released to Him once more.

From there she enters our world. From there she now waits for us, with joy and holy impatience.

Could any deny the greatness of the gift?

Thank you, Celeste, for saying *yes*.

There Fun is...

"...everything can be taken from a man but one thing: the last of the human freedoms – to choose one's attitude in any given set of circumstances, to choose one's own way."
Viktor Frankl

"Where we are, there fun is." That's our family's motto, and we try to live by it faithfully. No one can quite remember how we came up with it, but it suits our family to a "T." We say it captures the "Adamkiewiczy-ness" (say it with me, Adam-KEV-itchiness!) of our clan perfectly, and we hope that those who know us agree: "Where we are, there fun is." This is very appropriate for us, a family many would charitably refer to as "quirky." We have a way of looking for the humor in every situation. We love the absurd and silly, and we revel in nostalgia, the oddities of pop culture, and the way life can be so incredibly awful sometimes that you have to laugh in order to bear it. You just *have* to laugh!

My friend Katherine and I have labeled this thing called life "The Heinous Voyage." It's a trip you don't necessarily want to take, but you're on it, baby, so hold on tight and make the best of it. So we have. We've named a pet frog after 70s icon Charles Nelson Reilly, just to give you an idea how we think.

This is not an easy motto to live out many days, the least of which on a day when you have a child in the hospital. To live it out for many months of that is nothing short of a miracle, but we did our best.

Affability became a necessary antidote to the constant stream of misery. As we spent more and more time in the NICU, we realized we could, and should, approach this situation as we did any other in our lives. We knew we had pain to endure, and we could grit our teeth and drag the world down with us, or we could do our best to see the positive in everything. My husband, an optimist by birth, inclination, and determination was going to do his best to keep everyone smiling, even though this was the most difficult thing he had ever gone through. He was such a wonderful example to me. I, not so naturally positive, really needed his encouragement. With him by my side I strove to be kind to the nurses and thank them daily for caring for Celeste. I tried to be patient with the doctors when they had bad news to deliver. I smiled at the other parents and spoke to them when they seemed ready, encouraging them and silently praying for their babies. I attempted to see the best in the situation, to trust that God knew where He was leading us.

  We spent many evenings in the NICU sitting at Celeste's bedside and chatting with the nurses. We talked about where we went to school, discovering Celeste's primary nurse, Heather, had gone to my alma mater and even belonged to the same sorority. We talked about music, movies, and current events. We complained together about the choices in the cafeteria, acknowledging the strange attraction of the Hawaiian burger, which featured a thick, greasy patty topped with slices of ham and pineapple. We shared potty training stories and parenting advice with Rhonda, who had a three-year-old at home like we did. We listened to Heather, who was not much older than our eldest daughter, tell stories about her childhood and the roots of her secret fear of aliens.

And we laughed. Many nights we laughed and laughed and laughed, saying, "If you can't laugh in the NICU, where can you laugh?" We were so pleased to arrive there and find our favorite nurses caring for our baby, knowing that at least we would be smiling by her bedside as we spent time with people we genuinely liked. We were convinced she knew this: that her parents were with her and we were *happy*.

I convinced myself that Celeste knew we were there, that she sensed our moods. I did not want her to ever feel despair or fear. I did not want our sorrow to consume her. The nurses confirmed this belief, saying that their experiences told them the babies with the most pleasant parents fared the best. Wanting to do everything we could for Celeste, we buoyed our spirits during our time with her. We told funny stories. Aaron sang to her every day.

We knew, too, that Celeste needed parents who also cared adequately for themselves. The kindness of friends and family who prepared meals for us and helped with childcare made this easier, and we reminded ourselves that we must accept any offers we received. We went home for rest and tried to get enough sleep each night. We ate an occasional Hawaiian burger and took some time for recreation. We worked through the difficulty of such an idea and on Independence Day we gave up our daily visit to Celeste and spent the day at the lake with our other children. It felt so wrong to leave her, but the nurses encouraged us. They heralded the healing powers of the great outdoors.

They were right. We were refreshed by the water and wind, renewed by the time in the sun. On other days, I spent time with my best friend, seeing a movie, even getting a pedicure. I shopped with my daughters, doing "handbag therapy." I attended the graduation parties of my daughter's friends. Usually I did these activities while making excuses. I felt so guilty for leaving my baby. I felt so awful that I was trying to have fun while she was suffering. But looking back I realize I was doing my best to care for myself, and that was ok. It was more than ok; it was necessary.

Time off was required, balance was critical, and a sense of humor was indispensable. After sending so many disturbing updates and anxious prayer requests, I sent out this email on June 24.

Here's a quick story that I think will make you smile (nice for a change!) The other night Aaron and I were visiting Celeste and wondering when her heart will come. We realized next Wednesday, the 29th, is Aaron's grandma's birthday. So we decided to ask Busia, who died in October of 2003, to send Celeste a new heart on her birthday. The next day the phone rang. It was Purple Heart calling to set up a pick-up. On the 29th, of course. We had a good laugh saying, "Busia, we said a new heart, not Purple Heart!" But heaven knows we need the visit from Purple Heart too!

The PICU

"I say to God, my rock, why do you forget me?"
Psalm 43:10

Early in July Celeste was moved to the PICU, the pediatric intensive care unit. A number of things led to this change in accommodations. Celeste had tested positive again for RSV, and even though her symptoms were mild this time, they wanted her isolated from the other children. In the PICU she would have her own room. She had also tested positive for MRSA, a resistant form of a staph infection. These conditions were in fact the result of her long hospital stay. Indeed, we learned it was quite common, if not fully expected, that long-term NICU babies would suffer many infections. Some would even die from them.

The staff assured us that the transition would be easy, and that many parents reported they preferred the privacy that the pediatric unit offered. The unit was located only across the hall from the NICU. Her care would be much the same. The same cardiologists would oversee her care.

But there were many changes as well. Even though the unit was just across the hall, we discovered right away that things were done very differently. They had a different type of monitoring equipment. They had different methods of suctioning ventilator tubes. They had their own protocol for administering medications. And most difficult for us, the staff of nurses and doctors was completely new. As in the NICU, there were different nurses and doctors every day; here though, the staff doctor in charge changed weekly instead of monthly as they had in the NICU. We were overwhelmed. The familiar setting was gone. We had never minded that we were in a large room with other babies, because that meant there was always a nurse nearby if we needed help. (And Celeste always needed help, especially frequent suctioning.) Here we felt isolated and alone, and the nurses were strangers to us. We left behind the nurses we felt had become our friends. Here no one knew Celeste and, to add to our feelings of displacement, we now were repeating her history every day.

I missed the nurses of the NICU, and I wanted to take Celeste back. It was also difficult to be in a ward filled with older children. Even though Celeste had her own room, getting to it meant walking through the department and seeing all the other children in their beds. We frequently heard their cries as they called out to their mothers as they endured procedures. The little girl in the next room, her body withered by cystic fibrosis, died shortly after we moved there.

Something changed in my spirit shortly after the move. I was tired of being in the hospital. I was starting to give up hope that a heart would ever arrive. It was during this time that I told whomever would listen that it just had to end soon. I was not comfortable in the PICU, and I constantly felt out of my element and strange. Celeste, on the other hand, actually seemed to improve, albeit in small ways. They weaned down her ventilator settings, and even made one attempt at allowing her to try breathing without it. Her blood levels of oxygen were improving. Joanne, the transplant nurse, commented that she had never seen her looking better. The surgeon visited and said that even though Celeste had RSV and MRSA, she was looking so well that if a heart arrived, he would accept it. Everyone else was feeling positive, but I was weary and discouraged.

This note reflects my mood at the time.

> Well, good news and bad news. The good news is Celeste is doing very well. They have cut her prostaglandin dose in half, decreased her sedation and lowered the rate on her ventilator. The bad news is she has several new infections -- a staph infection (treatable with antibiotics, but resistant) and RSV again. Both of these are contagious, so they have moved her to her own room in the PICU. We now have all new nurses and doctors. This is so hard for us. We really felt comfortable with the staff in the NICU, and now that comfort is gone. They also reinserted an IV line today, because the other one had been in too long. Another OR procedure.
>
> Need I tell you that we are extremely discouraged? Fortunately they have decided not to deactivate her from the transplant list so that she can accrue days on the list. But if a heart becomes available they will have to consider if she is well enough to receive it. This has been one of those days when we look at each other and really wonder -- will it ever happen?
>
> I talked with the transplant nurse today and she confirmed what I've been feeling. It's true that

Celeste has had a harder path that most of the transplant patients they've seen. But on the other hand Joanne said she felt Celeste was really doing well (all things considered) and she really has a sense everything will be ok. A nugget of hope for me to hold on to.

I also talked to a mom who is taking her baby home tomorrow. When he was born seven weeks ago, they could not find a heart beat for 15 minutes. He was on ECMO (heart lung machine) for a week, had pneumonia and RSV, and they told his parents his condition was as critical as it could get. They could not believe he would recover, but he did. His mom attributed this to prayer. She said she trusted God and claimed a healing for her child when no one thought it could happen. Good advice. I'm trying to take it myself.

Hindsight tells me that perhaps I, as her mother, had an intuition that something was about to change in Celeste's condition. Perhaps when I had uttered the words, "This had to end," I was speaking from knowledge revealed only to my spirit. I was soon to see the true meaning of those words. Here, in the PICU, we began the last leg of the journey.

The Test

"Only a real risk tests the reality of a belief."
C. S. Lewis

July 11 was an ordinary day in the hospital. I arrived for a morning visit with my baby, not expecting anything new. Truthfully, I don't recall many details of that day. I imagine it was much like the others. I probably gave her a bath, soaking her bedding and trying not to rip out her ventilator in the process. I dressed her in an outfit that was not too restrictive considering her IV's and monitor wires. I was actually becoming adept at handling her with all the extraneous paraphernalia that was part of her life. I took a few breaks to pump breast milk for her feeding tube and to visit the Young at Heart cafe. It was probably a quite uneventful day, by and large, as far as days go in a hospital ward.

    I don't remember when I found out about a test that had been ordered for Celeste. I always talked with her nurse to receive an update on her condition, and as often as possible tried to pin down a doctor as well. This particular day I spoke with the resident on staff. A test had been ordered because someone had noticed something about Celeste, something so simple that her mother should have seen it first. Something so basic that nothing more high tech than a tape measure was needed to verify that there may be a new, very serious problem with Celeste's condition: her head looked small.

    Since Celeste had been intubated for most of her life, and since she was frequently swollen from head to toe, it hadn't previously been quite as noticeable. But that tape measure had confirmed what some nurse had suspected when seeing Celeste off the ventilator a few days before. Her head circumference, which should have grown four centimeters since her birth, had only grown a little more than one centimeter. An MRI had been ordered to get an accurate picture of her brain development.

I vacillated between mind-numbing fear of the worst and certainty that everything would be fine. After all, hadn't they done extensive testing to determine if she was "qualified" for a transplant? She had undergone numerous genetic analyses, ultrasounds, blood work and more. We had sweated it out hoping she would pass, and had been assured she was a good candidate. They had told us they would not do a transplant if her other systems were not functioning well enough to sustain her life. Since they gave her the green light, she *must* be in good shape.

I don't remember calling Aaron, leaving the hospital, or coming home to tell my kids their sister needed prayers; but that's what I did. Hoping for the best, I sent out this note.

> Celeste is doing ok today. She had a busy weekend, as they took her off the ventilator and then ended up putting it back in last night. She was just working a little too hard without it. We were surprised that they took it off at all. Her sats are better today and she was resting quietly when I went to visit earlier. The RSV is also cleared so in that respect she is doing well.
>
> We do (of course) have a prayer request, though! They are concerned that her head circumference is

not what it should be. Her height and weight have increased well but not her head measurement, so they are concerned her brain is not growing properly. Apparently it could be caused by her low levels of oxygen. They are doing an MRI to look at the brain more closely. It is possible that her head is just small or that it is growing slowly but it is also possible that she has brain damage. But it is also possible that somebody measured inaccurately! Her genetic tests were all normal, so the neurologists will have the last word tomorrow.

You know what to pray for.

It is going to be a rough night for us. We've had nights like this before, and let me tell you we are tired of them! But Celeste has always come through ok so we have to trust that once again she will be all right. The worst point of my day was when the doctor inferred that if there is brain damage she will be "disqualified" for the transplant.

"Disqualified for the transplant" makes it sound like she was an unlucky contestant on a game show, about to be booted off the stage with little more than a parting gift. Yet that phrase had the power to chill me to my very soul. It was simple. If she did not receive a heart transplant, she would die. That poor resident had the unfortunate task of telling me that the news I would receive the next day might very well be the worst news we could imagine.

Contemplating the death of your child is a little like contemplating the origins of the universe. It is mind-blowing, beyond imagining. It sends you to an emotional state of complete alone-ness, a sense of total abandonment. Physically, you are drained and weary, your very body tender with pain. Spiritually, you cry out to God, "NOT MY CHILD!" You know that sometimes children die, but never, *never* your child. It simply cannot be. Of course this night I asked why, repeatedly. I begged God for the best news and prepared for the worst. Would this news be that my daughter's death was a certainty? Could it be that I was right, that the ending of the drama was here, that it would be over soon? Would my prayers be answered? Would the answer be "no?"

It is true that I had asked for an end to my daughter's sufferings. I imagined this would occur through life-saving surgery. Now I became aware that perhaps the Lord had an answer to my prayers, but not in the way I hoped. Maybe He was saying *Yes, Cathy. I will answer your prayers. I will heal your daughter in the most profound way possible. I will bring her home to Me where she will never feel pain again.*

An answer to my prayers was indeed coming son. An ending and yet an extraordinary beginning.

Made-for-TV Moment

*"My God, my God,
why have you abandoned me?"*
Psalm 22:2

I know in my heart that the end of the story will be dramatic. I imagine a scene in which we receive a phone call in the middle of the night: "We have an organ!"

There will be commotion, excitement, concern. Celeste will be rushed to the operating room, and her tiny chest opened. They will remove her heart, her weak, damaged heart that should not be able to function because its deformity is so immense. Perhaps, later, they will show us this heart which, though imperfect, has served her so well. For now it will sit in a shiny silver bowl, lifeless, while they magically place the heart of someone else's baby into my baby's petite chest. It will begin to beat, and she will be pink, so pink. The surgeon will emerge from the surgical suite, exhausted yet victorious, to let us know that our Celeste is now ready to live for many, many years. We will weep with joy, and the dramatic story will come to an end. It will finally be over.

July 12. I am holding this dramatic ending in my heart when I enter Celeste's room. She is still, sleeping. I look at her charts, as always, the numbers there indicating an ordinary morning. She looks the same as she did last night. But nothing is the same.

I see the resident that has the information I need: the results of last night's MRI. She scurries around the nurse's station. Is she avoiding me? She certainly seems to be. Where is Celeste's nurse? Where is everyone? There are nurses everywhere, doctors making rounds, interns taking notes. But the PICU seems empty, quieter than usual. Everyone seems to be moving very slowly, very softly, and I am invisible. I ask whomever I see to find out the results for me, and they stare at me blankly, not really seeing me, not caring, not helping me, not hoping with me. Do they know, do they all know, the horrible truth I am about to discover?

"Profound brain damage." "No transplant." "Insufficient growth." "Multiple strokes." "No transplant."

"I'm sorry." "Massive retardation." "I'm sorry." "No transplant."

No transplant.

No transplant.

No transplant.

The resident is speaking to me, and I am watching her lips move, and thinking that she is young, so young. I am stroking Celeste's head, her tiny head. Her unbearably tiny head.

I keep my composure. I stand, by her bed. No one offers me a chair, or a drink of water, or a prayer, or a gun. There are no offers to call my husband, only one to call the neurologist, because *right now you need to talk to the neurologist, Mrs. Adamkiewicz.* No, in fact no one here calls me by name. I know they are only people, just like me, who do not know how to treat someone in a moment like this. But it feels as if they do not even respect me, and that they do not even know my name.

I am just the mother of the sick baby. The baby who is going to die.

Gethsemane

"Father, if you are willing, take this cup away from me; still, not my will but yours be done."
Luke 22:42

I headed to the NICU, not quite sure what I'd do when I got there. My daughter was going to die, of that I was sure. I needed to talk to someone who knew me, someone who could tell me I was dreaming.

I maintained my composure until I walked through the double doors. I saw Sunshine, Leroy's mother. She, of all people, could understand my pain;

she was waiting for a heart for her baby, too. The words spilled out in a jumble, "brain damage, no transplant." She tried to assure me that of course they would not abandon the plan to save my baby. Her eyes were wild with fear. If my baby could die, so could hers. She tried to comfort me but I knew it was over for us, that our families no longer shared the bond of a common solution.

Someone called my sister-in-law, and soon she was with me, and we sat together in an unused nursery down the hall. She was angry at the resident for the abrupt treatment I had received, determined to use her connections as a staff member to discover some new information, to somehow change the reality of the situation. She, too, loved Celeste. She did not want this truth any more than I did, and for a moment I believed she might be able to change it. Then reality returned, and I cried out with more anguish than I thought possible.

"Does God hate us?" I cried.

I wept with a passion reserved for mothers of dying babies. I never wanted to leave that room, desiring to remain there forever, because that's how long my tears would last.

"No! He doesn't hate us! He loves us!" she reminded me. She said more, but I don't remember her words. Those words were so meaningful to me. Michele was on her own walk with the Lord, and she was at a different place than I was. I knew her faith had grown because of Celeste, and that this moment proved that. Through Celeste's life Michele had learned to put her trust in God.

Eventually I calmed and the tears subsided. Soon Aaron and I were standing by Celeste's bedside as a head neurologist explained her condition.

There are moments when worldviews collide, and this was one of them. When we asked the doctor what he would do if this were his child, we were shaken by his response.

He shrugged and replied nonchalantly. "Oh, I'd let nature take its course," as if we'd asked him what we should do with the dying bug stuck to our shoe.

It was so obvious that to him, Celeste was nothing more than a list of figures on a chart. She was a substandard creature with no purpose. There was no meaning to her life. She would never be productive, doctors couldn't fix her: she was *nothing*. Her life and eventual death did not affect him. She would just be a "morbidity statistic" on the receiving end of a "negative outcome." Just some dead, useless, defective kid. No biggie. I was face-to-face with the secular message of the value of life and despised what I saw.

We should have been prepared for this when exposed to his cavalier attitude upon greeting us. He smiled: just another day at the office. "Why are you wearing a tie?" he said to my husband upon meeting him. I wanted to scream "He's wearing a tie because he rushed here from work when I called him to tell him his daughter was going to die, you idiot!"

In all charity, he *was* an idiot. He was far more educated than my husband and I put together, and his IQ and experience topped ours by far. But he was still an honest-to-goodness idiot.

I asked him how the doctors who evaluated Celeste for her transplant could have missed her extreme lack of brain development, and this is what he said:

"Look, I'm a neurologist. When I look at you, I see a brain and a spinal column," expressing that each specialist cared only about a particular system, that the cardiologists who cared for her didn't look closely enough at her nervous system.

In one of the proudest moments of my life, I told him this. "No, *you* look. I'm a mother." I pointed at Celeste. "When I look at her, I see a human being. I see my child." I was aghast at his lack of sensitivity and ignorance of the value of human life. He made the hardest day of our lives all the more difficult because although he had great intelligence, education and knowledge, he lacked the most basic understanding of all -- that each human life is precious.

    I wanted to be angry with him, but instead I was overcome with pity. He could not give what he did not possess. I prayed that someday he would receive a gift of understanding to equal his medical knowledge. What a blessing that would truly be to the myriad parents and patients that were sure to be in his future.

    Soon another doctor took his place, this time the head of the PICU. His white coat couldn't cover the loving and empathetic man that he was. His gentleness and genuine compassion shone through brightly, and to Aaron and myself he was an angel. He patiently sat us down and explained Celeste's condition. He reviewed MRIs with us, not growing weary at our repetitive questions. He told us he was sorry, and we knew he truly meant it. He told us to go home and rest, as doctors must, but he did not patronize us.

    Going home was difficult. How do you tell children that their baby sister is going to die?

    I do not recall the words we used, or even what the children said in reply. But I will never forget the sound of their weeping, the sight of my sons holding each other in comfort, my daughters huddled together, their shoulders shaking, eyes swollen. I will never forget the love that was present, how very tangible it was. I was so proud of them as they loved and comforted one another with abandon. We were shaken to the core with sorrow, but we were suffering together. A gift.

    This email was the hardest one I had to write.

Dear Friends and Family,

I have been sharing honestly with you all from day one, so here goes. I will do my best as long as I can type this out.

We received some very bad news yesterday. Celeste's MRI was abnormal, showing several areas of concern. Her entire brain is quite small, several areas are undeveloped, and she has suffered at least one stroke. With a 90% probability she is severely mentally retarded. Most likely this has always been the case, a birth defect that probably occurred in the first trimester of my pregnancy.

How did they not find this earlier???? They had to do tests before they would list her for the transplant, but somehow the ultrasound they did not show enough information.

The neurologist has already written a recommendation that she not be listed for transplant. We have not yet spoken to the head cardiologist on the transplant team, but it seems likely this will be the case. They will not do a transplant.

As you know without a transplant she cannot survive. We have not been "given all the options" yet, but the neurologist was very frank (painfully so) in saying if it was his child he would "Let nature take its course."

Are there words to describe our despair? We love her and want her so much. We have been through so much already it seems the suffering is unbearable. But yet I must say I just feel so honored to be her mother. She is a precious, beautiful baby. She was made in God's image, perfectly made the way He desired her to be. She has done so much in her short life. I just wish it could be different.

We cannot make it through this without your prayers. We want to do the right thing, the best thing for Celeste. We are seeking counsel to do that. Please pray especially for our other children and our parents, and don't forget the kind nurses who have grown to love her as well. And please pray for each other, I know you are suffering with us as you learn this information.

And when you pray thank God for His beautiful gift of Celeste.

A Birthday Party

*"Rejoice in the Lord always.
I shall say it again: Rejoice!"
Philippians' 4:4*

We had a beautiful day today with our daughter Celeste. She turned four months old today and we celebrated by taking all the children down to visit. This was so special as it was the first time our whole family was in the same room! We were able to take lots of pictures and even some video to remember this special time with her. She even had her long awaited date with Lauren's boyfriend that we've been promising her since she was born.

We received a bit more news about her condition yesterday. It turns out that her brain malformations are the result of the strokes she suffered, not a birth defect. Her brain was likely normal at birth and simply stopped growing adequately when the blood flow decreased. So the brain damage is secondary to her heart condition.

We also were told that no one will remove her from the transplant list unless we give the ok. We are now in the process of gathering all the information we need to make the right decision for her. Pray for us that we may have the gift of discernment. This is the kind of thing you read about in a magazine or a text book on social teaching -- not something you want to live through! But we are being called to "walk the walk" and we want to do it well, to really do the best, most moral thing for all involved.

Our pain is immense but so is our joy. That's why I started with a comment about the blessings we shared with our daughter today. I know you are all suffering with us and I want you to know you must share our joy as well. Every moment with our loved ones is such a gift.

It is Celeste's birthday, and we are having a party. There is no cake and no balloons, but there are plenty of children, which is what parties are all about, anyway. Celeste is beautiful in pink. We have dressed her up for the occasion, and her big sisters have selected just the right hair bow and socks to accessorize her ensemble.

It is not a birthday proper, measured in years, because when you are going to die soon every moment is a treasure. It is her four-month birthday.

As on the 14th of each previous month, her hospital bed is adorned with a sign announcing her age. This one is more elaborate than the others, which were drawn and tacked up by mom. This one was drawn with more care -- in fact, such painstaking artwork was never before seen on a birthday sign. Each letter is a different color. The shades are bright and joyous, accented by a sketch of four balloons. It is obvious this sign is special, a one-of-a-kind commemoration of a very special birthday. It was made by her daddy.

For the first time, ever, all seven of my children are in the same room. We take lots of pictures, and we smile and sing. Video cameras are forbidden here, but we use one anyway. Some of these rules are just plain silly.

Silly. We are very, very silly. There is much laughter, even authentic joy. Today, we have our baby girl, we have Celeste. We are together. We do not say aloud what we are all thinking: her next birthday will be her birthday into heaven.

Right and Wrong

"When we are no longer able to
change a situation...
we are challenged to change ourselves."
Victor Frankl

We now know for certain that Celeste is not going to live much longer. MRIs and measurements, neurologists and cardiologists. Everything leads to the same conclusion: Celeste is no longer a candidate for a heart transplant. And without one she will die.

It just seems right to seek counsel, so we do. A

friend contacts Mark Latkovic, the seminary professor we spoke with earlier. I ask for a meeting with the hospital ethics committee. We pray that we will do what is right.

What is *right*. I have always been a black and white person, someone who acts with conviction when I am convinced I must. This time I feel lost. Everything boils down to one essential question: if I allow my daughter to die, am I in fact killing her? Wouldn't a good mother do anything and everything to protect the life of her baby?

As I wrestle with this question I turn to my dear husband, who is making these decisions with me. We pray together, as has been our custom throughout our marriage, not in words, but in silence. He holds me and I hold him. We cry. I touch his face and he holds my hand. At dusk, we sit in the backyard together, looking up at a glorious blue sky with pink popcorn clouds, and ask God what to do. He is silent, too.

We open the pages of the well-worn *Catechism of the Catholic Church* housed on our living room shelf. For Catholics, the catechism serves as a guidebook on matters large and small. Its passages speak clearly on prayer and the sacraments, on the teachings of Jesus and how to live them out in today's world. Several sections describe "end of life issues." We read and pray quietly. We talk a little and we look into one another's eyes. We pray the Rosary with the children. *What should we do?* Is there really a decision to make after all? The doctors have effectively sealed Celeste's fate. They will not perform the surgery that will save our daughter's life. But what do we do now? Do we allow ventilators and medicines to prolong her life, or do we remove them and let her die? If we choose the second option, are we any different from the neurologist who recommended we "let nature take its course"?

Everyone seems to have an opinion, and strangers and friends feel free to share them.

A few point to a little girl who lives nearby, one who has been on a ventilator for several years. They think that Celeste will be fine if we keep supporting her artificially, not taking into consideration that her heart will fail eventually. Another boldly asks us if Celeste will choke to death on her own saliva if we stop helping her breathe, not realizing these are questions no mother should have to answer about her own child. One email reader sends information on a "miraculous" supplement that will surely rebuild Celeste's damaged brain. I know she means well, but her exhortations that we push for the transplant cause us only pain.

Some friends, thankfully, seek only to comfort and encourage us. Of particular help are those who have lost children themselves. One beautiful couple, whose son died soon after birth, takes us to dinner and allows us to pour out our confusion and sadness. They do not offer false hope or condemnation, only love and support.

We take in all the opinions, hold onto one another, and pray some more. Now it is time to hear the "experts." Our scheduled meeting with the hospital ethics committee arrives. By this time, I have gained a sense that I know what to do, that I have the moral framework necessary to make a good decision. We have done our best. I feel in my heart I have the all the information I need, but nonetheless, I have requested this meeting, and it seems there may be another reason for it.

It is an intimidating group. Present are the head of the NICU, a cardiac surgeon, our social worker, a psychiatrist, and several others. One is a woman, a mother, I can't remember her profession but I can tell by the look in her eyes (she is overcome with empathy) that she is not a doctor. We sit at a large conference table in an unused room of the NICU, each of us serious and anxious to get this over with. Then an amazing thing happens. I begin to speak, and they begin to listen.

I had not entered the room with an agenda. In

fact, I hadn't really planned what I would say, but I quickly sense that I have been given an unusual opportunity. Celeste's story begins to be told. I explain the situation to everyone there, I tell them how distraught we are, how we feel things could have been handled better. I ask them why they didn't make measuring the heads of infants standard protocol. I ask them why this had happened. They probably offer some answers, but as they are inadequate they are also forgettable. Realizing that I really do have their attention, I proceed to tell them about the treatment we had received from the head neurologist. I want them to know that if they care about ethical treatment in this hospital, they need to know about this man and how he is failing to provide it.

Something begins to shift in the room. It becomes obvious that I am no longer seeking input to make an ethical decision. I am providing it. I begin to sense that some of these people have no clue about life! Sounds awfully bold, doesn't it? But as I speak about my daughter and our beliefs about the beauty and value of her life, it occurs to me that many in this room do not share those beliefs. "Quality of life." They have no idea that that phrase is offensive to me. They don't know that our spiritual considerations are far more important to us than concerns about how "normal"

Celeste could be. So we tell them.

Unlike the neurologist who delivered our bad news, I have the grace to look around the room and see not nervous systems, not hearts and lungs surrounded by flesh and bones, but *people*. They are professionals. They are intelligent and educated, hardworking and competent. But at the end of the day they are just like me: they are just human beings, imperfect, suffering human beings. I have a true epiphany. They do not realize that their own lives are valuable not because of their achievements, but simply because they are members of the human family. Perhaps they do not know that they, that I, that Celeste, that every child they will ever care for has inestimable value for one reason.

Our value is not in our doing, but in our being.

As I glance around the table, I try to look at these souls through the eyes of Christ. They are men and women; some young, idealistic and anxious to succeed, some at the twilight of their careers. Different races are represented, different faiths, different cultures.

Excitement stirs in my heart, and I want to shout at them. *We are all important! Our lives are sacred. I am not here just to advocate for my daughter, but for YOU! Your lives have meaning beyond your* *accomplishments. **All** lives have quality. We must seek to connect with one another, to serve, to love. We mustn't fear looking silly, or failing, or being sued.*

We must take a radical step. We must depend on each other.

I wanted to hold their hands in mine and tell them they were loved. I wanted to shake each of them by the shoulders, to slap them. I wanted to throw my arms around them and hug them and ask them why they were here, where they had come from, and where they hoped to go. I wanted to beg them to truly value life – the great gift of life.

Of course I did not act on most of these feelings, but I pray they influenced my words and increased their effectiveness. I don't know if their hearts were changed that day, but I know one thing. Mine was.

Some were still mumbling things about surgical risks and cost of care while we filed out of the room. But I did see the mom wipe a tear from her eye, and that psychiatrist had leaned forward and moved his head from side to side, asking lots of questions. David, our social worker, approached us on the way out. "They needed to hear what you said," he told us, "some more than others."

Then it was only our family left in the room, Aaron, Michele and me. Feeling triumphant, I picked up a stuffed teddy bear that was one of a pile in the corner. "I'm taking this home," I announced, and my sister-in-law agreed that I must. It was ridiculous, but it felt like a statement, and I was in a mood for statements. I knew Celeste would be proud of me.

I knew those reading my emails felt adrift, as unsure as about what was right and wrong as I had been. I wrote to them.

> We have spent the past week gathering lots of information about Celeste's condition and what we should do next. We have consulted our pastor, a moral theologian, and the ethics committee at the hospital, in addition to the staff of doctors including her cardiologist, neurologist and surgeon.
>
> Unfortunately there are no medical solutions to Celeste's heart condition. The surgeon feels she is a poor surgical risk due to her brain damage, which is extensive and profound. If she survived surgery (a transplant or otherwise) the long-term prognosis is not good. In short, there is nothing more that can be done for her.
>
> We have spoken to the wonderful people at hospice and some very kind ICU doctors who will be helping us along the way. Most likely we will begin by removing her ventilator and the prostaglandins, as these are the treatments that cause her the most discomfort. Now our goal is not keeping her alive, but making her as comfortable as

possible and treating her with the utmost respect and dignity.

I have a few very important things to tell you all now. First of all, I do not want any of you to feel that your prayers have not been answered. God is always faithful, and He always gives us what is best for us. We all wanted Celeste here with us for many years, but that may not be God's plan for her. Celeste has done so much in her four months here. She has touched so many people and will continue to do so from heaven! Our hearts are breaking as we think about letting her go, but she belongs to Him anyway. Do not despair! Please keep praying, about everything in your lives! God loves us so much. He has blessed us so greatly through Celeste. And your prayers have worked miracles. Celeste may not live, but it is a miracle that we are surviving this. That is due to those prayers.

I also want to express that in no way are we basing any decision on "quality of life" for Celeste. I have never liked that phrase. To be honest, Celeste is suffering far less than Aaron and I are right now. We are not ending her life. We are not letting her go because she is not perfect. We would care for her no matter what and we know ALL people are beautiful reflections of God's perfection, no matter what defect they may have. We were very careful to consider the teaching of our church on this, a teaching we believe to be true and beautiful. Those of you who know us well know we are strongly pro life. But to prolong the life of one whom God is calling home is humanistic, not Christian. We know that sometimes God calls His children home when they are tiny. Thinking about this gave me more peace. If Celeste were 90 years old we would not be doubtful about anything. We would say she had a good life and that we should not put her through unnecessary pain. The same is true for our little baby. She has indeed had a good life. She has never offended God with the tiniest sin. She is perfect and pure and wonderful. What a blessing.

So now please pray for a peaceful passing for our dear Celeste. It is difficult to say how long this may take; of course it could be hours or days. Once again it is in God's hands. You know how much we need your prayers now. Thank you for being there for us.

The Seventh Moment

Part Two

"Every promise has been fulfilled for you, with not one single exception."
Joshua 23:14

I am up early, and the whole world seems to be glistening. It is extraordinarily beautiful, and I feel in awe of everything— the sunshine, the dew on the grass, the midsummer blossoms in my yard. Many details of this morning are now lost to me, but this I remember: there is beauty everywhere.

Our pastor says Mass for our family in our parish church, the church where I was baptized and Aaron and I were married. It is a wondrous, intimate Mass, with just our family and a few close friends. We pray and we sing, "Be not afraid, I go before you always. Come, follow me, and I will give you rest."

I sit in the front row and clearly think, "I am so glad I am Catholic. I love this church. I love the Eucharist. I feel so close to Jesus, and I am so thankful I can receive Him today." Viaticum --"strength for the journey." Adults receive the Eucharist under this title when they are dying. Celeste will not receive Communion before she dies, but somehow I feel God has allowed me her share, her strength for the journey. I know I will need it.

Father accompanies us to the hospital in our van. I am chatty, comfortable, even a bit excited. We talk about the sacrament of confirmation that Celeste will receive today, and we tell Father her new name will be Catherine. We talk about the graces that will flow, about the way the day will pass perfectly in the will of God. Our talk may seem pious, but we are not theologians discussing religious theory; we are merely simple believers. I thank Father for saying Mass for us, and tell him how peaceful I'm feeling. We talk about this reality: if we really believe what we say we do, if we *really* believe, we must rejoice. We must rejoice for our Celeste, today like no other day.

> In many ways I feel just like I felt before the birth of each of my children. I am anxious and a little scared. I wonder how much it will hurt. I wonder if the pain medication will be adequate. I wonder how long it will take. But I also know that when it is over it will be a new beginning. There will be a new baby. A new life. This time a dear daughter being born into heaven, where she will never know pain or disappointment. I can't wait to get there with her, where I know Our dear Lord will give me back every moment with her, and then some. Like my children keep reminding me, she is indeed the lucky one.

When we arrive at the hospital, we bathe our baby girl. She grimaces, as she always does, as we lather her hair and rinse her chubby body. We dry her gently and rub her with a touch of lotion, and we dress her in her baptismal gown. She is really wearing it this time; it is not just lying on her still body, she is wearing her gown, and her mother has dressed her in it. Despite the contraindication of the ventilator tube, we also manage to tie the matching bonnet under her chin. She is beautiful.

The hospital room is tiny, but we cram our whole

family and several close friends inside to witness her confirmation. Lauren, her sister and godmother, holds her while Father anoints her. She is sedated, but when he tells her to "open her eyes" and receive the gifts of the Holy Spirit, she obeys. A hush falls on the room.

As the sacrament is completed, we know that Celeste is now an "adult" in the eyes of the church, a fully incorporated member of the Body of Christ. Unlike most of us, she is sinless and pure. She, without doubt, will enter Heaven immediately upon her death. She will be a saint.

Friends and family say their goodbyes to her. We, with the help of hospice nurses, make molds of her hands and feet and cut locks of her hair. We take lots of photographs. Finally, the others leave, and we are glad, anxious to have her to ourselves. We dress her in a pink terrycloth sleeper. The nurse gently removes her ventilator tube, and I am startled at its apparent simplicity. Such a tiny tube, so easily removed, has kept my daughter alive for so long. And now it is gone.

All of the tubes and wires are removed, the monitors silenced, and for the very first time, I hold my daughter up to my cheek, her head on my shoulder. It has been a long time in the making, but it is finally here. My seventh moment.

Birth

> "It is in dying that we are born to eternal life."
> Prayer of St. Francis

Aaron holds his youngest daughter close to his heart, and I am overwhelmed with love for both of them. I know his suffering is of a different nature than mine. He is her father, her protector, and he must let her go.

He holds her in the air, as he has all of our children, playing "jet-pack baby." He only holds her up for a second, because she is weak, doll-like, her head wobbly as a newborn's. He sits in the rocking chair with her and reads, tenderly and steadily, his favorite story. Shel Silverstein's "The Giving Tree" was never more bittersweet.

In the background there is music playing. We listen to Disney Princess lullabies, and then pop princess Kelly Clarkson. "Breakaway" has been number one on the charts for literally Celeste's entire life. The lyrics seem to speak clearly of Celeste; we have dubbed it her song.

Rocking with her Daddy, she is beautiful to us, but truly not very pretty. Now that the tubes and tape are gone, we can see the scabs on her pale cheeks. The top of her head is tiny, totally out of proportion with the rest of her body. Her stubby fingertips, which had taken on a clubbed appearance in recent weeks, are beginning to turn blue. Her color is bad, and she looks battered, almost bruised.

We are completely enraptured with her.

Her grandparents and siblings visit, taking turns holding her close, but we only have eyes for her. As I was during childbirth, I am focused on the transformation. I do not want to miss anything.

I feel a desperate need to be alone with her, and Aaron graciously leaves, although I know he is afraid she will die in his absence. A pain surges through me that I did not expect. She is leaving me, and I think once more of the many moments we should have shared, but did not. Of the memories we will never make. The grief surges in waves, and I finally begin to weep. I am holding her and rocking her and whispering her name, again and again. I am making her promises. I promise I will not forget her. I promise I will embrace my life fully, without bitterness, with thanksgiving for the great length of life I have been given, which she has been denied. I promise to write this book.

Aaron comes back in, and I feel at peace again.

She does not seem to be suffering, but we can tell she will leave us soon. Her breathing is shallow, her skin mottled. A nurse checks her heart and nods; it will be soon now.

At 3:33 that afternoon, Aaron looks at me, his eyes pleading. I know he needs to be holding her, so I hand her to him, and she lets out a tiny breath, a gentle sigh.

She is gone, and I am overwhelmed with grief and joy, awe and amazement. I have seen a glimpse of heaven.

The hospice nurses encourage me to hold and cuddle her as long as I need to, telling me I will know when it is time to go. They are right. At just the right time I place her on the hospital bed, her soft flannel blanket wrapped snuggly around her. I kiss her goodbye and leave that room, and I do not look back. I know I will see her again.

Celebration

God saw she was getting tired
And a cure was not to be.
So He put His arms around her
And whispered, "Come with Me."
With tearful eyes we watched her suffer
And saw her fade away
Although we loved her dearly,
We could not make her stay.
A golden heart stopped beating,
Hardworking hands to rest.
God broke our hearts to prove to us
He only takes the best.
Author unknown

Printed on Celeste's memorial cards

My dear friends,

"God Who is mighty has done great things, and holy is His name."

When I was going through my labor having Celeste, I thought it was odd that this paraphrase of Luke 1:49 kept going through my mind. It doesn't seem to have much to do with suffering or children, so I wondered why it seemed so important.

Now I think I know.

Celeste was called by God from her conception to do a mighty work for the Lord. I know she has touched so many lives, and will continue that great work from Heaven.

Our dear Celeste was confirmed this morning, taking the name Catherine. As Catholic Christians we believe the sacrament of confirmation imparts the gifts of the Holy Spirit in a new and powerful way. It also makes one an adult in the eyes of the church, a fully incorporated member. Catherine is of course my name, and I was named after St. Catherine of Siena, who did so much to teach about the church and bring unity. But we decided Celeste's patron would be St. Catherine of Alexandria, a young martyr who gave her life for Jesus, just like our Celeste.

Celebration

> Celeste Marie joined St. Catherine and all the angels and saints and her Blessed Savior at 3:33 this afternoon after only about an hour and a half off the ventilator. She did not suffer in the least, dying peacefully in the loving arms of her father.

After stating the specifics of Celeste's funeral arrangements, I extended an invitation.

> We are so sorrowful but so filled with joy, the joy of knowing our dear daughter is with Jesus!
>
> Come celebrate with us!
>
> P.S. Wear pink! The color of joy and Celeste's favorite color

We knew it would be difficult, but we hoped many of our friends and family would truly make Celeste's funeral a celebration. We were not disappointed.

Hundreds visited the funeral home, where I proudly showed off my angelic baby. I had always avoided the funerals of children myself, so I knew some would not choose to come - it was just too difficult to see a baby in a casket. Of course even I was a little afraid to see her. Would her appearance be disturbing to me?

When I approached the casket the first time, I was overcome. She was gorgeous. She was wearing a dress I had bought before her birth; a beautiful satin and organza dress in cream with a pink rosette. The pink shoes on her feet were purchased the day before. (I'm sure the nice lady at the children's clothing store couldn't imagine why I wept as she rang them up.) Her tiny hands clutched a pink rosary. Her skin was no longer mottled and blue, her wounds were successfully covered. She looked like a beautiful doll, and I kept fighting the desire to scoop her up. I was so happy, because I knew she was even more beautiful than this in Heaven.

The night before the funeral, we prayed the Rosary, not for Celeste's soul, because we knew she did not need prayer, but for the intentions of the many who had prayed for her during the course of her life. My heart surged with joy as the room reverberated with the sound of those Hail Marys! We also played Celeste's song once again. "I'll spread my wings and I'll learn how to fly, though it's not easy to tell you goodbye...Out of the darkness and into the sun, I won't forget all the ones that I love." There were no dry eyes.

Person after person approached Aaron and me as we stood by her casket, their eyes swollen, their hugs tight. We were overwhelmed as friends and strangers embraced us and shared their grief and love. It was extraordinary.

The day of the funeral was stiflingly hot and

Celebration

humid. Our church lacked air conditioning, and as the church filled I worried someone might faint. Later some told me they had never been more physically uncomfortable in church; my brother even joked that Celeste was just giving us all a taste of where we did not want to end up to keep us on the straight and narrow.

Funerals are always difficult, and our pastor assures us that the funerals of children are the worst. The "why" that everyone is asking seems to dominate the service, taking on a visible form in the anguished faces of the mourners. These funerals are an occasion for doubt and questioning fear, a temptation to despair. I prayed Celeste's funeral would be neither, but only a time of joy.

As I sat with my daughter as she lay in her casket, waiting for the church to fill with friends, I touched her face and was startled. She was cold, so cold, cold on a day when ice had trouble keeping cool. It became real to me that she wasn't even with us anymore. She was so far away from this nasty, blazing world, so far away. A hot breeze blew through the open doors of the vestibule, and it seemed so sad that this was the first breeze to ever waft through her hair. But I knew the breezes of Heaven were far more refreshing.

A Father's Gift

"When a man finds that it is his destiny to suffer, he will have to accept his suffering as his task; his single and unique task...No one can relieve him of his suffering or suffer in his place. His unique opportunity lies in the way in which he bears his burden."
Victor Frankl

The church is full, and Mass is about to begin. It is time to say our last goodbye to our little girl. Aaron and I gather with our children around the tiny white casket, and each of her siblings places a pink rose there. She is wearing a bracelet from Children's Hospital, given to her by Grant, a staff member and new friend. He had been wearing it himself, committed to doing so until she received a new heart. I did not know until a few days before her death that he too had lost a baby daughter years earlier.

Aaron places his gift to her there: a pink CD with "Breakaway" on it. On it is written "I will always remember you in this song. Love, Daddy." Lukie adds a lollipop.

I gently tuck a pink blanket around her. I know she does not need it, but I need to do it. My gift to her is a note I have written, for I know my words are my heart. No one else has read the note. No one else needs to; it is a secret between us.

The funeral director gently closes the lid, letting us know it is time for the processional to begin. No pallbearers or gurneys are necessary for the tiny box, and he offers carry it forward for us. Aaron shakes his head. He will do it.

The casket is small and light, but I know it is the heaviest thing my husband has ever lifted. As our friends and family sing, we carry her to the altar, and Aaron, weeping, places her at the foot.

For a moment, I can see her standing there, a

pretty young girl in a white dress and veil, waiting to receive her First Holy Communion. Then time shifts, and I see her again, a lovely young woman in a white dress and veil, waiting to receive the Sacrament of Matrimony. It is a culmination of all these moments, future moments that will not be. Her father has given her away at the altar. He has given her away.

Later I am told that many found this moment to be heart wrenching and profoundly moving. In this one act so much was contained. Like St. Joseph, who is never quoted in the scriptures, Aaron was a silent witness of a father's love. His action touched many hearts.

At least one conversion followed. A friend told us later she had been away from the Church for eleven years, since the death of her beloved brother. As she watched Aaron give Celeste back to God, something changed in her spirit. For the first time in over a decade, she sang in church. She had come home.

Another acquaintance that was deeply affected by Celeste's life and death began classes to study the Catholic faith. When she joined the church at Easter of 2006, she said that our family had played a role in her conversion.

Aaron gave his best gift back to God, and God kept giving and giving and giving.

The Harvest

*"How wonderful it is
that nobody need
wait a single moment before
starting to improve the world."
Anne Frank,
Diary of a Young Girl*

At Celeste's funeral, we said goodbye to our daughter. The next day, I realized it was time to say goodbye to the many who were praying for her.

My dear sweet friends,

Celeste's funeral was beautiful. As many of you know, she looked absolutely exquisite, like an angel.

We were so touched by the number of friends and family who came to the funeral home to be with us. As person after person approached Aaron and me, we felt like George Bailey in the final scene of "It's A Wonderful Life." We are so blessed to have such wonderful people in our lives! Thank you!

Her funeral Mass was so precious to us. Our pastor did such a beautiful job in comforting us and reminding us all of the realities -- that Celeste is truly a saint in heaven. We must rejoice in the midst of our suffering.

So now, it is time to say goodbye to all of you. This is so difficult to write. I know a very special experience is coming to an end. Sharing with you has been painful, for me and for you, I know. Many of you have told me that these emails have been important to you, and I am so grateful for that. I hope I have not shared too intimately, and I know that at times they have been difficult to read. But I hope you do not regret going on this journey with us, because I know I have no regrets about sharing our hopes, our fears, our suffering and our joy. It is always a risk to love. You took that risk with us, and although the end of the story was oh so sad, I think we are all better people having experienced it together.

I would like to share one more story. As you know, Celeste's confirmation patron is St.

Catherine of Alexandria, a martyr from the early church. On Monday her grandmother, who is a stamp collector, received in the mail a pamphlet about a series of stamps from Malta. Their subject? St. Catherine! On the pamphlet was a short biography of St. Catherine, from which we learned that she is the patron of philosophers, theologians and preachers. How fitting for our Celeste! We have begun to feel that part of Celeste's mission, in addition to being an advocate for suffering children and their families, is to bring believers closer to Jesus. We have received so many emails and letters, and heard so many personal testimonies, about how knowing Celeste has drawn them closer to Christ. We have already received four testimonies of regained faith!!!

So I am reminding you all to pray to St. Celeste Marie, asking for her intercession in your lives. She will not forget you. She knows how you loved her and prayed for her throughout her life. And to my dear Christian friends of other faith traditions, who may find this odd -- please don't. Think about it this way. You had never met Celeste, but recognizing her as your sister in the Body of Christ, you interceded for her, prayed to Jesus on her behalf. Now she wants to do that for you! She wants to whisper your prayers into the ear of the Lord, and she can, because she's sitting on his lap! While recognizing that there is no mediator between God and man but Jesus Christ (1Timothy 2:5), we can surely acknowledge that we are all called to intercessory prayer for one another (1 Timothy 2:1). And who is more alive than our dear Celeste, who is with Jesus today!

Right now we are all riding high on emotion, and we say we will not forget our Celeste, or what she's taught us. I beg you to remember her. I wept so hard yesterday thinking about her life, about how much she suffered. We don't need to go over every detail again, but that's what I did yesterday, and the pain was deep. My heart ached every day of her life because she suffered and I could not even nurse her to comfort her. But I want you to know this. Her suffering was worth it if even one soul comes to Christ because of her! And I believe that's already happened! One email we received stands out in my mind. It was the most beautiful thing I have ever read. Because of Celeste's life and death the author said she had regained her faith! How precious that note is to me, one of many I will hold in my heart forever.

In one of my early emails I said perhaps it wasn't Celeste whose heart needed mending, but ours. How true that was. You may recall that her heart was two or three sizes bigger than a normal heart. It truly was, wasn't it? And like the song at Mass said, "Here I am Lord. Is it I, Lord? I have heard you calling in the night. I will go, Lord, if you lead me. I will hold your people in my HEART."

Please contact us to let us know how she has touched you. Yes, let us know about your miracles!

I thank you and I love you
Cathy

My heart was full as I wrote this final email, because I knew that something extraordinary was coming to an end. I would miss hearing from those who were praying for us, and I would miss writing to them. I would miss the notes from strangers that confirmed my belief that Celeste had left her mark on the world. Receiving these notes verified my dearest hope – that Celeste had not suffered in vain. Her life had been meaningful.

During the last weeks of that summer, I was not disappointed. My mailbox was full of joy.

I've delayed sending you this response to your last email because I've been trying to sort out my thoughts about Celeste's life. You asked us to let you know how she changed our lives, well, I can tell you that she had a profound effect on mine. I never got to physically see her or hold her, but I felt about her the way I feel about my three precious grandsons, I loved her dearly. Her too short life caused me to re-examine my own faith and beliefs and brought me to the Lord in an even closer and stronger way than before. I always thought my faith was strong, but in these last four months, I've learned what true strength of faith can do and it will be the pattern for the rest of my life. I do find myself praying to her daily and I can feel her listening. Amazing what a strong saintly figure that tiny baby has become to so many of us. Sorry if I've rambled on, but I did want to share my feelings with you. Thank you both for your wonderful examples of faith and love. It's meant a great deal to me and to my family.

Your beautiful words of God's love through His saints (such as little Celeste Marie) were so inspiring and even though I don't know you personally, you have touched my heart.

Please accept my condolences and prayers for you and Celeste. The Emails I received from you have been heart rending, and heart lifting at the same time. Thank you for sharing Celeste's life, in some mysterious but significant way, with me. I will pray for her intercession.

I thank you from the depth of my heart for sharing your dear sweet, beautiful, little Celeste with us. I love her.

I do not know anything else about your family-- how many children you have, where you live etc. But I do know you have acted with immense grace and courage to share your beautiful baby and your journey with all of us. I am so deeply grateful.

What a loving God who shared Celeste with us all. What blessed and loving parents who shared Celeste with us all.

I, too, have been touched by this sweet child and her faith inspiring family whom I have never met. It is through the sharing of our most difficult and faith testing times that we can witness the power of our Awesome God. Please thank them for generously sharing this difficult personal experience with such eloquence and profound faith, it is truly inspiring. Some of my life's recent challenges have left me with a heavy heart and many questions about my faith. Celeste and her family's journey, which I feel fortunate to have shared through email yet am certain is exactly as God intended it, provided just the perspective correction I needed.

With renewed faith, God Bless Sweet Celeste, his newest little angel...she has truly helped to heal my heart.

I shared your July 20, 21 and 22 emails with four of my closest friends. I wanted their thoughts because it seems that you have in your emails the making of a book that would help other parents in similar circumstances. Here is what one said to me...

"Those are the most special parents I have ever come to know. Their words will stay with me forever and yes I think they could help others in their hour of darkness. Please let them know how much they have to offer others from their love of their precious daughter. And know that we all pray for their peace.

Celeste was here for a purpose and maybe learning to let go for many heartbreaking parents was her purpose. Let them know they have much to offer."

Each message left me feeling that Celeste had indeed achieved a mighty purpose. I sensed too that her work had just begun.

Signs

"I won't forget the ones that I love."
Kelly Clarkson

Celeste has been dead for a week, and I am sitting in the sunshine of my back yard. It is gloriously sunny, temperately warm. I am peaceful, missing her but still shocked by the fact that her life is truly over.

Of course as I sit in the Michigan sun I am thinking of her. Exactly one week since her death, my arms feel as if she has only been gone for minutes. I know that life is now different for me, that my perceptions will be forever altered by what I have experienced.

Mostly, I miss her. I am sad. Sometimes, when I allow myself the time, I can *feel* her. The thoughts of touching her skin, stroking her hair, kissing her cheek are more than memories; they are tangible, real Celeste, and they are here now, not just moments in the past.

I do not ask for messages from heaven, but I receive one. A small white butterfly lights on my knee. For several moments, it sits perfectly still, allowing me to examine its paper-thin wings. There, in perfect detail, amazing and stark and wonderful, is painted by nature a tiny black heart. Blinking, unbelieving, I take it in. A heart. Celeste's symbol. A gift from her to me on a summer day, a sign if ever there was one.

She has not forgotten me.

The Portrait

"Rest assured that in her dying,
in her flight through
darkness toward a new light,
she held you in her arms
and carried your closeness with her.
And when she
arrived at God,
your image was imprinted on her
joy-filled soul."

Molly Fumia,
A Piece of My Heart:
Living Through the Grief of Miscarriage,
Stillbirth, or Infant Death

Soon after her death I knew I wanted a portrait of Celeste.

We had many photographs of our baby, a scrapbook full of prints, some happy, mostly sad. There were few that were truly pretty, none that showed just Celeste. Each photo of her also contained the image of at least one form of the medical machinery she had required every day of her life.

I have always loved photographs. My home is filled with them, and I've more than my share of scrapbooking projects at various stages of completion. Each event in the life of our family had been meticulously documented with pictures -- each birthday, First Holy Communion, and graduation. Storage boxes are full of charming photos of my children at all ages, their beautiful faces preserved in dozens of snapshots. There would be no such pictures of Celeste.

I began to envision a special picture of my baby, one that would capture her beauty as she should have been in life, but was not. Her beauty as it certainly was now in Heaven. I could only be with her in my dreams, and my power to conjure up a satisfactory visit was sorely lacking. I wanted an image of her with the Lord, where I knew she was. It never seemed right to merely visit the place of her body's burial. Was *she* even really there?

I made few cemetery visits. What mother could bear the thought of her baby entombed in the cold, hard ground? I did not allow myself to dwell on images of decay and darkness. I told myself that Celeste was Incorruptible, like the saints I had read about, who, when exhumed, showed no decomposition, but only beauty. It is possible, after all.

Celeste was not in a graveyard, anyway. She was on the lap of her Savior, enfolded in purest Love. She was blissfully learning the mysteries of the universe, not wasting time on this dismal planet learning the useless skills of speech and ambulation. She spent her time conversing with Therese and Anthony and Catherine, never bored with the speeches of politicians or salesmen. Her little hands touched the wings of angels, not to be burdened with the drudgery of work. Mythology? Wishful thinking? Pious imagination? Or reality?

I chose, and still do, to believe. I urgently desired an image of Celeste there, in that Heaven. Never mind that I knew no artist, amateur or professional, atheist or believer, who could help me bring this image to life. I asked Celeste to help me, and she did.

Years earlier I had, at the coaxing of a dear friend, taken up the habit of making a weekly holy hour. A holy hour, which one need not be holy to do and often lasts less than an hour, is a devotion in which Catholics adore Jesus, Whom we believe to be truly present, body and blood, soul and divinity, in the Blessed Sacrament— the bread which a priest has consecrated. In short it is time spent with Jesus. I was not always faithful in my observance, but I did find that any time I spent with Jesus was always a blessing to me. Fairly regularly I visited my parish church, where the Host was exposed in a beautiful monstrance on the altar all day one day per week. After Celeste died I found myself drawn there even more. I knew she was with Jesus, and if He was resting on the altar, my Celeste was right there too.

I returned from church one Tuesday and came home to find the mail waiting for me. Nothing important, just the usual bills and advertisements. I absentmindedly paged through a few catalogs, glancing at the pictures of various books and artwork in a Catholic media offering, when a beautiful image caught my eye. It was a representation of Mary, an image known as the Immaculate Heart, unlike any I had seen before. The Immaculate Heart is a popular image, one

The Portrait

that many artists have interpreted, but this one was unique. The face was extraordinarily lovely, almost childlike. The colors glowed; it was realistic in style with a softness that drew me in. I knew immediately that this was the type of portrait I desired. I scanned the catalog description and quickly discovered this was a new work by Seattle artist Tracy Christianson.

  Thanks to the Internet, once again a close ally, I found Tracy's website within minutes, and was thrilled to find out that not only did she specialize in religious art, she also created commissioned portraits! With tears in my eyes I sent off a note to her, explaining what I was seeking. I knew she was the artist I was looking for, and I was right. She promptly responded and within days was working on a colored-pencil portrait, which was the first time she combined her two areas of expertise. Normally, commissioned portraits were essentially copies of photographs that were sent to her. This time she would be creating an original artwork with an image of Jesus and a picture of a baby, my Celeste, which was not a copy of a photograph but an interpretation based on a number of images.

  Tracy was as kind as she was talented, and she patiently talked with me many times so she could design the portrait just as I wanted. We had many conversations about Celeste, and what her life had meant. I felt that Tracy was a kindred spirit. She truly understood the importance I placed on the portrait, and I knew she was making its creation a priority. She told me that she prayed to Celeste for inspiration, and I was confident she would receive it.

The end result is magnificent. It is an image of Jesus that is warm and tender, pleasant and loving. Celeste radiates the beauty that she should have had in this life, and certainly has now in Heaven. I believe it clearly depicts the scene of the pair of them before she was born, and is a representation of their reunion. It comforts me immensely.

The original portrait now hangs in the cry room of our church. Our hope is that it is a comfort to all who have lost loved ones, a reminder that we all hope someday to be cuddled like babies on the lap of our Savior. I, for one, can't wait.

Memories

"I answer the heroic question 'Death, where is they sting?' with 'it is here in my heart and mind and memories.'"
Maya Angelou

On most days, the great gift of my faith buoys me against the dark despair that threatens to overtake me. On others, my grief becomes a consuming black sea. I feel vulnerable and sensitive, like a walking, fresh wound too delicate to bind, too raw for even the best

Physician's touch. I struggle to survive, to breathe. I am so deeply immersed in grief that I fear I might never surface. I feel sorry, so sorry, for myself.

On these days, my hunger for memories consumes me.

Attempts at consolation fail. Some come from well-meaning others, most from my own heart. "What about that family who lost their twelve-year-old? Can you imagine how hard *that* would be? They had to watch him suffer, and they had all those memories of when he was well."

"Do you know about M.? She's been on a ventilator all her life. I think she's three now. She will never be able to interact with her family. Don't you know Celeste is better off?"

"I feel so sorry for Mrs. P. She and her husband were married for 49 years. How ever will she manage without him? Her grief must be so horrible. At least you didn't have Celeste in your life very long."

I am angry. Angry at the Man in the portrait, the one holding my baby close to His Heart.

I am jealous, jealous even of the friend who lost her two-year-old in a tragic accident (at least she had a healthy child for two years, and his death was quick.) I am jealous of the woman I read about who lost her daughter to cancer at age three. Three years with her!

Memories

She brushed her hair. She heard her speak. She fed her ice cream. Oh the worlds they had that I was denied! The bitterest of agonies: that mother saw her daughter smile. Her daughter looked into her eyes and smiled at her. Celeste's eyes, although beautiful and blue, with the longest lashes I had ever seen, never locked with mine. My greatest suffering.

Of course my sufferings were so much greater than any one else's. We all want the world to know that our cross is the heaviest. I resented the stories of others in which I was told I should not feel so bad. Of course I should feel so bad. I should feel worse than any other human being who has ever lived, even the mother of that guy who hung on that cross. Of course I should.

Grief manuals instruct me to "remember the good times," to concentrate on the pleasant memories of my loved one.

There is a problem.

There are no pleasant memories.

I search for images to comfort me, and I find emptiness. In her life there was only suffering, constant unrelenting suffering. I search and I search, and I beg God for memories.

He sends me a few.

She is doing well today, and I am rocking her

slowly in a broken down chair in the NICU. I glance at her monitor and her oxygen levels read 100%. There is warm sun shining into the darkness of the room. She sleeps in my arms.

I am nursing her for the first time, not knowing there will only be a handful of opportunities for us to share this experience. Her suck is not strong, but she is trying, and for five glorious minutes her cheek is soft on my breast. I am feeding her; she needs me. There is hope.

And my favorite memory. She is not yet born. I am round and full with her, and she rolls gently in my belly. I am home alone – so rare – and as she sleeps beneath my heart I fold my family's laundry. I am listening to a popular song on my daughter's computer. "Tell me why don't we go, somewhere only we know..." I am content, blind to suffering, waiting for birth, waiting in delicious ignorance.

They are only a few memories, but they are mine, and I guard them jealously. I will fight resentment all my life. I will succeed in my fight, because I choose to. I will remember the supreme importance of the life of one little girl, and I will dwell not on sorrow but on joy.

Might I be lying to myself? Perhaps. Suppose

my faith is a myth and my beliefs about suffering a lie. Do these beliefs then lose their power to console? Hardly. I cannot consider the alternative, that beyond what we see there is vast nothingness, and all that is real is grief and despair. I choose faith. A false comfort? Maybe. I acknowledge that I do not have all the answers. But like Pascal, I will make the wager. The odds are too good, and anyway, who can choose a horrible truth over an illusion that consoles? The playwright Pirandello tells the story of a woman whose son has died. Not able to face this terrifying fact, she invents a reality in which he lives, one in which he has just gone away for an extended holiday. Others debate the value of convincing her of the "real" reality, but ultimately she stays in the world she has created, a world in which she is safe, and her son, her life, is well. Is she crazy? Or is the "real" world crazy for not seeking the beauty and solace of illusion?

Is Christian faith just such an illusion? Am I wrong about what is real? Even if I am wrong, and I am willing to bet my life I am not, telling myself that suffering is redemptive is my peace. I cannot live this life without that balm. I do not believe anyone can.

Mourning In Technicolor

"The agonies, the mad midnight moments, must,
in the course of nature, die away."
C.S. Lewis, A Grief Observed

As my first year of grief unfolded, I came to an inescapable conclusion: children die. Indeed, sometimes children *must* die. This side of Eden, death is a certainty, one even the youngest cannot escape. *Children die*, and this fact leads to a wondrous realization: their deaths are unfathomable gifts of mercy. An extreme paradox, to be sure -- must we lose the most innocent to gain grace for the wicked?

The death of a pure soul is bittersweet. Experience taught me that sometimes these pure souls, these children, are taken from this world not as a punishment to those of us left behind, but as a reminder of what really matters.

We have become so evil in our day. If children never died, would there be *any* saints in heaven?

Celeste's death began to bring me hope rather than despair. I began to look at the world through different eyes, eyes at first clouded by tears and then cleansed by them.

Our lives are precious gifts meant to be tended with care. The world I had once viewed in black and white began to take on brilliant shades of gray. I sought to see the gifts others had to bring, and I desired to know my own. It became easier to forgive the faults of others, and in myself, when I reminded myself that each of us here is a reflection of God, a unique person with a mission from Him, a vessel of His grace. Life became at once miraculously simple and marvelously complex.

There were no black armbands in the Adamkiewicz household. Instead, we mourned in Technicolor, figuratively and quite literally. The walls of our home became a canvas on which I purged my pain. Looking back, I'm aware it was done unconsciously, but now I see the reason for the rainbow that emerged there. Within months of her death, our kitchen was painted an extravagant orange. Soon after, a bathroom glistened with the brightest shade of apple green. I purchased unique art from my new friend Patti, whose knack for combining color, form, and the written word took my breath away. I sought unusual items at art fairs and boutiques that, I often joked, "spoke to me." I was especially charmed by hearts, butterflies and dragonflies. I sang, poorly but with spirit, in a community theatre musical. I spent time writing. I kept my promises to Celeste. The pendulum had swung to the farthest reaches of sadness, and now I was hastening it back to a place of joy and beauty. On the way back to normalcy I decided, quite consciously, to stay that swing somewhere left of center. There had been more than enough blackness in my life, and now I chose color.

My choice to some may seem gaudy, inappropriate. But from where I sit, the hill on the other side of the valley of death is covered with a field of flowers, and I'm taking time to fashion a bouquet.

I spent more time thinking, just *being*, than I had in years. I read books, some heady and some not -- mostly not. I thought about classes I had taken in college, in which I was challenged to appreciate and interpret "serious fiction."

As a college freshman, I read Tennessee Williams' *Field of Blue Children* for the first time; now I reread it. It inexplicably attracted me on both occasions. At first reading, I certainly lacked the talent to accurately gauge its meaning, but I felt Williams had created Myra in my image. Angsty and tormented, this college coed, who seemed to have everything, sought "something still further to give the night its perfect fullness." She wrote verse to comfort herself, finding that "whenever the rising well of unexplainable emotion became so full that its hurt was intolerable ...it helped her a little to scribble things down on paper."

"Words are a net to catch beauty!"

When I read those words at seventeen, I thought I was looking in a mirror. My writing provided me with a means of reconciling pain and beauty, a tool for processing desire and fear. Like Myra, I longed to discover a "field of blue children", a transcendent garden of cobalt blossoms glistening in the moonlight, that would accept and embrace me. Even with my limited skill at deciphering fiction, I knew Williams was describing that place in our lives in which we are hopeful and blissfully naive, that creative place in which anything is possible.

Re-reading the story two and a half decades later, my critical skills, though not greatly evolved, see a bit more. Where then I saw only the innocent yearnings of youth, now I see a sexual tension and a desire for danger, reminding me that our fields are deeper and more complicated than we may think. More importantly, I see the field of blue children as a place one escapes to when life requires us to *feel*.

Nothing causes one to feel more than death. Celeste sent me back to my field of blue children, and it is exactly as I had remembered it. For that I am forever grateful.

The Sea

"Earth has no sorrow that Heaven cannot heal."
Unknown

Throughout the trial that was Celeste's life and death, the Lord used my imagination to bring me comfort. He, who created it, knows it is vivid indeed! I have accomplished much growth, achieved much solace, by paying close attention to my thoughts and dreams, by visiting that place in my soul where He reveals Himself. That special place He has created in each of us for His indwelling. A corner of our souls where we are free to create and dream, where we are innocent children with a fresh box of crayons. A portion of our hearts where we can glimpse Heaven if we allow ourselves the indulgence and trust in His grace and mercy.

When my suffering is most intense, the Lord allows me to see Him, in the eye of my mind, as He will be when we meet. It will be such a sweet reunion! I can feel His arms around me. I can feel His Love piercing my heart and melting all the sorrow it contains. I stay in His arms forever, because in the miracle that is Heaven that is the only time we have: forever. And then He shows me my Celeste.

She is radiant, effervescent, glorious. He allows me every moment I was denied with her on earth. At times I see her as she was, a tiny baby, perfect in form, but untouched by the pain that she endured every moment of her earthly life. Sometimes she is a toddler who walks unsteadily into my waiting arms, resting a head of tawny hair on my shoulder. At other times she appears as a child of five or six, a joyful child who runs to me with abandon. Most frequently I see her as a young woman, beautiful, so beautiful, who smiles at me

The Sea

and tenderly holds my face in her hands, knowing I have longed to see her but assuring me, without words, that she has always been with me.

We link arms and our Savior draws our attention to a sight almost beyond the imagination. It is The Sea. Like the seas of earth, it is beautiful and deep, glorious and vast. It holds mysteries of creation so miraculous, it will take eternity to comprehend. It is The Sea of Souls. The Sea of Souls who are in Heaven because of Celeste's cooperation with God's grace. Celeste who caused people to pray, to believe that their words with their Father would be heard. Celeste most certainly brought people, of their own free will, back to the Son.

Then Jesus takes me by the hand and gently coaxes me to witness another sight. I gasp in surprise. I truly was not expecting this. There, as beautiful as the first, is another sea. This one, too, is large and blue; pure and mighty. It is *my* sea. The Sea of Souls who are basking in their Savior's love because of me, because I fulfilled the purpose for which I was created. Because our Father is so good, heaven is filled with such seas. But there is room for so many more; there is room for a multitude of seas! How thrilling to think of their grandeur! What an honor to consider that God wants His precious children, here on earth, to bring one another to these seas.

Each day I remember that with God's grace, I am headed for the shores of those spectacular seas. I will be reunited with my little girl and I want you, too, to meet her. But first we must challenge one another with a question, one that I ask myself each day:

How deep will our seas be?

Acknowledgements

This book is the work of my heart, but I did not write it alone. My sincerest thanks to:

My husband Aaron, who taught me the meaning of unconditional love. You have my heart, both broken and blessed, forever. Honey, I know you miss our baby girl. We'll see her again someday.

My children, Rachel, Lauren, A.J., Joey, John and Luke, and my future sons-in-law Christopher and Giovanni. You are the best gifts I have ever received. May you always remember that your stories are as amazing as Celeste's. I love you.

My parents, Lawrence and Joan Klimchalk, my brother Chris, and my mother-in-law Bernice. Through you I learned the meaning of sacrifice, commitment and generosity. Mom, thank you for telling me I could be anything I wanted to be. I know you meant it. Dad, thank you for saying "I love you." Chris, thanks for reminding me the power of "don't worry about it." Your trust in the Lord inspires me. Mom, ("Grandma Bea") thank you for treating me like a daughter from day one.

My friend Katherine Lennon. *Friend!* You have been a friend to me in all the ways that matter most. Hang in there, the "heinous voyage" will certainly end with a safe landing on beautiful shores.

The doctors, nurses, chaplains, hospital staff and hospice workers of Children's Hospital of Michigan, including Joanne Dupuis R.N, Dr. Thomas Forbes, Rev. Marilyn Bahena, David Allasio, Grant Whittlesey, Heather Olah, R.N., Rhonda Stewart, R.N., Kim Stewart, R.N. and especially my dear sister-in-law Michele. You comforted and cared for Celeste and us during her life and death, and for that I can never repay you.

The staff and volunteers of Gift of Life of Michigan who do so much for the families of organ donors and recipients, and who work tirelessly to share the truths about transplantation. Learn more about their work at **giftoflifemichigan.org**.

My email emissaries, especially Dan Czarniecki and Mike Lemieux, who started the prayer chains that bound us together. Thank you for selecting "forward."

The many precious souls who shared Celeste's life through the windows of their computer screens, most of whom I will never meet. This is your story, too.

Our extended and spiritual families, especially our homeschool friends and the community of faith at St. Sebastian Church, led by our pastor and friend Fr. Jeff Day. The prayers, meals, friendship and support you provided nourished and sustained us.

Dr. Mark Latkovic, who compassionately helped us make the most difficult decisions. Thank you, too, for believing in this book and helping it come to fruition.

Contributing artists Tracy Christianson and Patti Monroe-Mohrenweiser. Tracy, I am in awe of the beautiful portrait you created. It is truly a glimpse into heaven, and I treasure it more than I can say. Patti, your cover art expresses so well what is in my heart, and I am charmed by the butterflies that grace the pages of the book. I am amazed at the way we were brought together. Patti, you say it best: "It's a God thing." I hope many will be blessed by the work of these two talented artists by visiting Tracy at **tlcportraits.com** and Patti at **beyondletters.com**.

Those who read my manuscript thoughtfully and offered advice, encouragement, and praise, including Bishop Earl Boyea, Rev. Marilyn Bahena, David Allasio, Fr. Jeff Day, Dr. Mark Latkovic, Dr. Bob Fastiggi, Kathy Fastiggi, Patti Monroe-Mohrenweiser, Ann Mulligan, Katherine Lennon, Jeanne Lewandowski, M.D., Patti Mitchell, Maria Housden, Patti Armstrong, Kimberly Hahn, Janice Edwards, Joanne Dupuis, R.N., Kim Stewart, R.N., and Debbie Herbeck.

My editor and new friend, Cheryl Dickow. Once or twice in a lifetime, if we're lucky, we meet someone who makes all the difference. You're that kind of person. You make me feel like I fit in somewhere, and I hope I do the same for you.

Those who will read Celeste's story, carry it in their hearts, and live out its message. God who is mighty has done great things for *us*, and holy is his name!

Please visit **brokenandblessed.com** to share how you've been blessed by Celeste.

Printed in the United States
200067BV00006B/220-372/A